PoMoSexuals

PoMoSexuals

CHALLENGING ASSUMPTIONS
ABOUT GENDER AND SEXUALITY

edited by Carol Queen and Lawrence Schimel

CLEIS
PRESS

Published in the United States by Cleis Press Inc., P.O. Box 14684, San Francisco, California 94114.

Printed in the United States.
Cover design: Scott Idleman/BLINK
Text design: Frank Wiedemann
Logo art: Juana Alicia
First Edition.
10 9 8 7 6 5 4 3 2 1

Library of Congress Cataloging-in-Publication Data

PomoSEXUALS : challenging assumptions about gender and sexuality / edited by Carol Queen and Lawrence Schimel ; Kate Bornstein, preface.
       p.   cm.
    ISBN 1-57344-074-4 (pbk.)
    1. Gays. 2. Gays—Identity. 3. Homosexuality. 4. Bisexuality. 5. Gay communities. 6. Postmodernism—Social aspects. I. Queen, Carol. II. Schimel, Lawrence.
HQ76.25.P66   1997
306.76'6—dc21

For Eve Tetzlaff, birthmate and friend.
—L.S.

For Robert, without whom it would just be theory.
And in loving memory of James Campbell, Esq.
—C.Q.

CONTENTS

Acknowledgments

Almost any book, and the anthology in particular, benefits from the generous advice and support of many people who assist in their individual ways. We are grateful to all those who helped make this project a reality.

Foremost, to our publishers Frédérique Delacoste and Felice Newman, for years of pushing at boundaries and for patience above and beyond the call of duty

To Kate Bornstein, for living boldly and for writing the preface.

To Dorothy Allison and Pat Califia, intellectual godmothers to this project.

To Kim Airs, Susie Bright, Michael Bronski, Jo Eadie, Mike Hernandez, Keith Kahla, Richard Labonté, Michael Lassell, Leah Lillith, William J. Mann, Scott O'Hara, Shar Rednour, Tristan Taormino, and Dr. Jerry Zientara for moral support, enthusiasm, and advice at various stages.

To Robert Lawrence, for inspirational and supportive acts too numerous to mention.

And of course, to our wonderful contributors, for those words they have written and have yet to write, and for their patience with us and our editorial whims.

QUEER THEORY AND SHOPPING:
DICHOTOMY OR SYMBIONTS?

KATE BORNSTEIN

Don't you just love irony? Especially when the irony involves you as its subject? This preface is a case in point. Here I am writing for this incredibly innovative, challenging, and queerly entertaining transgressive anthology at a point in my life where I seem to be leaving off being queer at all. Uh huh, I'm finally approaching the full stride of my life's girly-girl phase. Never mind I'm scant months away from turning fifty, fact is I'm much more interested in fashion than I am in politics, or even ::*gasp*:: queer theory. I'd rather have a femme buddy than a butch lover—what's that about? Maybe it's queerly appropriate after all that I'm writing for this book. I should tell you now: This is my first ever preface, so it may tend to wander. But that's gotta be appropriate for a book about the deconstruction of previously deconstructed sexual and gendered identities, no?

I really like this book, by the way. Honest. I'm not just saying that cuz someone's paying me to say things like that or anything. I like it because it's filled with stories and ideas written by people who are doing the unexpected, even above and beyond the quotient of unexpected acts required for one's queer membership card. But enough about this book for the moment; let's get back to me and why it's me who gets to write this preface.

So, okay, here we go. In a nutshell, I used to be a het guy who did the gender-change thing and became a grrl, a lesbian grrl at that. Then, after my female lover became a guy, I stopped calling myself a lesbian. Being a lesbian had become too complicated. Calling myself a lesbian managed to offend just about everyone, so I began to call myself a dyke. I thought I was really hot stuff because I wrote books about this kind of thing and came out in all sorts of big-time media, but my recent nationally-televised confessed crush on megastar David Duchovny signaled the beginning of the end of any status claims I had on high queerdom. (No, he hasn't called yet; I'm still waiting by the phone. I figure it's because he just got married and doesn't know how to call me without upsetting his wife.) This girly-girl stuff is new to me. It's almost embarrassing. I wanna go shopping, but I'm not. I'm sitting here at my computer trying to preface (is that a verb?) this book that brilliantly exemplifies queer theory, when queer is one of the farthest things from my mind. A good scarf, that's what I'm looking for.

My crush on David Duchovny has made me feel somewhat traitorous to the queer movement...that is, until I read some of what the people in this book were going through. I mean, wow! Now I don't feel so weird. I feel downright normal.

How about you? Ever wonder if you're the only one who doesn't quite fit in one of the sanctioned queer worlds? Like, are you really a lesbian? Are you really a gay man? Maybe you fall outside the "permitted" labels, and maybe you're the only one who knows you do, and so you feel a bit guilty? Well, I've got news for you. You're not guilty, you're simply postmodern. Isn't that neat? If you don't believe me, all you need to do is pick up this book and start reading anywhere. Really. I keep a copy in my bathroom because that's where I do a lot of my wondering. From revelation to analysis, from XX to XY and back again, PoMoSexuals is the literary amusement park we've all been hoping exists someplace. Carol Queen and Lawrence Schimel have found Oz, and they've asked some of Oz's leading citizens to tell us what it's like in the Emerald Kingdom. (Carol Queendom?)

Wait, wait, a preface isn't supposed to be an ad for the book, is it? And even if it is, then what if the book is about how to avoid all the "supposed-to's" in life? Would a silly preface fit in? I don't know. Anyway, this book isn't going to need any advertising. My bet is it's going to be on reading lists of queer studies courses all over the world, because it says in plain language and great stories what the heavy-hitting theorists have for years been trying to say in knee-deep academese. Yeah, this book can take care of itself, so let's get back to me.

Growing up in the 1950s, my role models started out with Shirley MacLaine and Audrey Hepburn. As a boy, that made me queer. Sure, I went through a period of wanting to be James Dean and even Leonard Nimoy, but I justified those times as my baby butch dyke phase—still pretty queer for a boy. Then when I went through my gender change, I looked for all the strong grrl types like Jodie Foster's Agent Starling and Michelle Forbes' Ensign Ro; that was considered queer by most cultural standards, but quite politically correct within the lesbian community (unless ya took into account that fact that I used to be a guy). Then I recently went trash bleach blonde, and I've come around to modeling myself on characters played by the likes of Mira Sorvino, Lisa Kudrow, Geena Davis, and Patricia Arquette. So now I sort of pass for normal. What a strange feeling that is!

But no matter who my role models have been, no matter how I've done my hair, no matter what particular twist I've gotten my genitals into, there's one thing I've always been a sucker for: ideas, concepts, and situations that fry my brain until all I can do is laugh. Like the concept of gender: All my life, I've been taught that gender is something essential, something we're born with. Well, for the last decade or so, I've become increasingly convinced that gender is some sort of social construct. That fries my brain, because it flies into the teeth of nearly everything the dominant culture has to offer on the subject. Maybe when I die, some- one's going to dissect my brain or some other organ and they'll find out it really was organic. I dunno. I don't care. I'm still looking for a good scarf. Pink. With repeating patterns of gold tubes of red lipstick. I can't be bothered with plowing through heavy theory. If I'm going to look at queer or postmodern theory, I need stories and pretty pictures. I need to be seduced into thinking about this stuff, because frankly it's too scary to look at without some promise of laughter at the end of the read, some playfulness as a reward to all the painful self-inquisition.

Well, playfulness is what this book is filled with, thank goodness. It's got great stories with a lot of brain-frying laughter. Here's one: Let's say you're a nice lesbian separatist who becomes a professional dominatrix and then falls in love with a male-to-female transsexual grrl and then you decide to go through a gender change of your own, become a guy, and realize you're a gay man. Well, how do you go about setting up your sexual liaisons? Believe it or not, the answer's in this book.

Or, let's say you're a nice Kinsey-Six gay man. You never had sex with a woman. But you wanna try, just because. How do you go about doing that? Uh huh, the answer's in this book.

Here's another one: You're a woman, born with all the medically-sanctioned grrl equipment, and you wanna jerk off with your own dick, but you don't want any kind of chemical or surgical intervention, you just wanna stroke your own cock and feel it. Yeah, that's in this book too: several times!

Too prurient for you? Okay, how about word games? How's this: Is it possible, do you think, to be queer when you haven't had sex in years? Or how about this one: Are words themselves a danger in the defining of community? Can we solve the problem of suffocating identity politics by allowing anyone at all to define the identities being politicized? Or would a better solution be the abandonment of politicized identities in favor of the politics of values? This book has all that stuff and more.

Then again, maybe that's too heady, huh? Okay, back to sex and gender. Say you're a woman, at least everyone sez you are; and you don't wanna be a guy, right? But your biggest turn-on is gay men. And you figure a way to completely satisfy yerself and your gay male partner as well. How could that be? Read on, cuz that nifty little conundrum is in here too.

Me, I think that situations like those are exactly what we need to stretch our brains beyond the banal. I think that if we want to grow at all, spiritually, intellectually, emotionally, individually or even as a race, however we want to grow, we need situations like these to tease our reluctant, recalcitrant, and (let's face it) lazy little selves into some growth. That's the way I've lived my life: I've followed the parts of myself that have made my brain fry every time I've thought about them. It's also how I shop. I mean, sometimes I buy something for myself that's really wild. Something I'd never dream of wearing, but for a split second once I've got it on in the store, I think to myself, "Wow, am I ever cute!" But it's a dangerous kind of cute, right? I mean, I'm not about to wear whatever it is right out of the shop and into the street, but it's something I know I can kind of grow into. So, I go ahead and spend my rent money or max out my cards to get whatever it is, and I take it home, and there sits my fashion purchase for sometimes months, while day after day I think about wearing it. I think to myself: Who would I need to be in order to wear that? And, am I ready to stretch myself into being that just for the sake of being really really cute? And once I get to that particular question, the answer is well, duh, obvious: Of course! And that's what reading this book is like. It's sort of a Rodeo Drive for the soul. In fact, I dare you to read any one of the pieces in here and remain exactly the same person as you were before. At the very least, you'll know you're not the only one who's weird.

So, okay. That's all I have to say.

Omigosh, I've written a preface. It's the first one I've written, and it's been kind of like literary foreplay. If it was as good for you as it was for me, then by all means keep on reading! I did, I enjoyed the heck out of it, and now I'm going shopping.

INTRODUCTION

While emceeing the 1996 Lambda Literary Awards
Ceremony, lesbian comic Suzanne Westenhoffer called for a
new term to replace the lengthy and cumbersome yet politically correct tag currently used by and for our community: "Lesbian, Gay, Bisexual, Transgendered, and Friends."
She suggested "Sodomites."

It's certainly more succinct, and is actually less glib than
it seems upon first reflection, for that is what most people
assume LGBT&F actually means, anyway. It's worth consid-
ering, though it probably won't be embraced any more
quickly by those who still feel contentious about using the
word "queer."

Only in the nineteenth century did doctors and
voyeuristic social scientists began splitting people up
according to sexual orientation, drawing boxes around us
that many of us later, through our commitment to identity
politics, embraced and reinforced. What we have been
called has helped to construct who we were, whether the
terms were the doctors'—homosexual, Urning, "sexually
intermediate type" *(Sexuelle Zwischenstufen)*—or our own:
homophile, gay, lesbian, LGBT&F. Even words laced with
opprobrium (fag, dyke, queer) have been co-opted and used
against the hetero world, serving to bind and configure us
in our divergent lives. Once named, language has shaped us,
both nurtured and circumscribed our identities.

This constructing, shaping power of language mated

with essentialism—the tendency to ascribe abiding charac-
teristics on the basis of gender, orientation, or some other
quality—begat a fractured, fractious community within
which queers risked being ostracized if they did things the
"wrong" way or with the "wrong" person. No wonder we
are and have been so contentious about language, paying
attention to and arguing about inclusion and exclusion, the
terms we use for ourselves and our communities and the
ones which are used about us. No wonder many of us have
desired to escape the corral of language completely.

We don't propose that "pomosexual" replace LGBT&F.
We're not interested in adding another new name to the
slew we already have, though we acknowledge the useful-
ness of having one name by which all LGBT&Fs might be
called. "Pomosexual" references homosexuality even as it
describes the community's outsiders, the *queer* queers who
can't seem to stay put within a nice simple identity. We coin
the term to situate this book and its essays within and in
relation to the LGBT&F community. It is in every way an
artifact of, and in many ways a backlash toward, this community—or rather, to certain assumptions widely held
within and/or about it, essentialist assumptions about what
it means to be queer. We react against these assumptions in
the same way that in the art world Postmodernism was a
reaction against Modernism.

We write "backlash," "reaction against," but in fact there
could have been no Postmodernism without Modernism
to serve as its foundation. Similarly, we have been nurtured
in the gay; the gay and lesbian; the gay, lesbian, and bisexual; and the gay, lesbian, bisexual, and transgendered communities—without them, we would not be who we are,
would not be measuring ourselves against their standards.

These communities serve profoundly as our homes, our intellectual and political sources, even as we chafe to make them bigger and even less restrictive.

Postmodernism looks for art and meaning sourced in the mundane, in wacky or arcane juxtapositions, in low as well as high culture. In this it bears some relationship to camp, queerdom's own ironic social theory, which developed to let us criticize (particularly heterocentrist) relations of power. Postmodern thought invites us to get used to the Zen notion of "multiple subjectivities"—the idea that there is no solid, objective reality, that each of us experiences our reality subjectively, affected (or influenced) by our unique circumstances. This mode of thought encourages overlapping and sometimes contradictory realities, a life of investigation and questioning as opposed to essentialism's quest for the One Truth, the innate quality, indubitable facts on a silver platter, the answer to everything.

What happens to identities based on essentialist thinking when we begin to challenge fixed notions of gender identity, binary thinking, monosexuality? When we want names that acknowledge and help shape how various we are? When gender dysphoria becomes first a sex toy or a way of life, then an inspiration to think about the mutability of everything we have been taught to consider fixed? When we insist on identities that embrace our diversities and refuse to gloss them over?

The problem with any ascribed and adopted identity is not what it includes, but what it leaves out. Indeed, there are so very many ways to live in the world, countless sources of affinity, that our sexualities and gender/identities only go so far in describing, constructing, and supporting us. To combat the "cosmic aloneness" that is integral to being human, that aching awareness that no one can truly share your experience (paralleling the koan that one can never stand in the same river twice; the water that made up the river at that moment is forever gone once the moment has passed), we form communities and subcommunities grouped around shared history and interests, links of family and ethnicity, religion and sexuality, anything which makes us feel more connected to others and less alone.

Queers have a special aloneness in addition to this universal isolation: our difference from the cultural mainstream, and our general absence from the world and worldviews in which we grow up and live. Hence it is especially important to create space for ourselves in the world and the culture, to feel connected through the names we give our communities. The more communities we overlap in, the more links we feel to other people—and the less isolated. The '70s and early '80s saw a flowering of sub-identification within our communities: gay Mormons, anarcho-lesbian-feminists, gay Republicans, lesbian mothers and gay dads, lesbian sadomasochists, gay veterans, gay Sierra Clubbers...a limitless list that continues to grow and expand as we connect and recognize connections with our fellow humans.

Twenty years ago, identity seemed self-evident. There were men, and there were women. Some were gay and some were straight. Bisexuals and transsexuals were suspect because their position on the sexual spectrum implied transition, disloyalty, or kinky hedonism; because their position on the gender spectrum implied permeability of a membrane we were all raised to see as solid; and because, when all was said and done, even homosexuals and women mostly believed that biology was destiny. The dissent had only to do with what that destiny might be.

But bisexuals never shut up and went away. Omnisexuals and pansexuals began to dot the landscape. Women who had been born with penises sought to attend the Michigan Womyn's Music Festival and, slowly, other dykes began to agree they ought to be there. Men born without cocks and balls fought doctors for permission to get gender reassignment surgery even though they intended to begin new lives as gay men. The practices and language of S/M began to move out of the dungeons and into the discourse. Lesbian butch/femme reasserted the erotics of gender in what was supposed to be an androgynous future, keynoted by what de Beauvoir called "the miracle of the mirror." Phrases like "butch bottom" began to dot the personals. Anyone with eyes and a brain could see categories breaking down, assumptions rupturing, clear-cut identities going the way of the Berlin Wall.

Hence the "pomosexual," who, like the queer s/he closely resembles, may not be tied to a single sexual identity, may not be content to reside within a category measurable by social scientists or acknowledged by either rainbow-festooned gays or by Ward and June Cleaver.

Pomosexuality lives in the space in which all other nonbinary forms of sexual and gender identity reside—a boundary-free zone in which fences are crossed for the fun of it, or simply because some of us can't be fenced in. It challenges either/or categorizations in favor of largely unmapped possibility and the intense charge that comes with transgression. It acknowledges the pleasure of that transgression, as well as the need to transgress limits that do not make room for all of us.

The anthology is an especially postmodern sort of book, making space between its covers for many writers of diverse points of view. This book, in particular, is concerned with analyzing and making cultural space for our individual sexualities, gender identities, and lack of identities. We share an identity within the *über*-LGBT&F community without letting our allegiance to these communities or identities serve as shorthand for all of our political or personal opinions—or our sexual practices, explorations, and mores. We neither can nor seek to cover in appropriate depth all of the many issues and questions this book raises (not to mention those it merely glances at in passing, or those it does not, due to restriction of space and time, address at all); nor do we attempt to create a "canon" of transgression or have the last word in the discussions we hope to provoke.

We do hope this book makes people question and rethink their own identities—not necessarily with the intent of changing them, but of better understanding other identities. We hope it pushes people who live more or less nonproblematic lesbian and gay lives to look more clearly and compassionately at their neighbors for whom things are not as simple. We hope this book makes some people feel less alone.

We learn and live through our stories; when something wonderful happens in our lives or we arrive at some profound revelation, our impulse is not to hoard it but to share the story with our friends and families, with our communities, so they can recognize themselves— and know us better—in the telling. This book shares some stories of investigations, of assumptions overturned, within our communities and our lives. We hope these stories inspire and entertain, that they make you think, that they raise questions.

We pomosexuals are the queer's queers, the ones who will

not stay in the boxes marked "gay" and "lesbian" without causing a fuss—just as we all burst out of the boxes the straight world tried to grow us in. At bottom, we want our communities (whatever they are or are not called) to embrace and support more of us.

Carol Queen and Lawrence Schimel

BEYOND DEFINITIONS

Alfred Kinsey, author of the famous Kinsey Scale, refused to use any of the terms describing sexual orientation—words we use as nouns, as if they describe something indubitably defined—in any way except as adjectives. To him, sexual behavior could be described; sexual identity was not fixed.

But the charged building blocks of sexual identity politics, while integral to essentialist ideas about who we "are," are not the only words that are open to contentious interpretation or which threaten to shape our experience or understanding. As Greta Christina notes in "Loaded Words," what we think a given word means may differ a little or a great deal from what you think it means. When our interpretations, colored by elements too varied to count, don't match, what effect does this have on our conversations, our identities, our politics?

LOADED WORDS

GRETA CHRISTINA

I have an ongoing argument with my best friend about the word "bisexual." She claims, quite vehemently, that words are useless unless they have a specific meaning that is generally understood by everyone using them, and therefore we need to agree on a single definition of bisexual and stick to it. (Not surprisingly, she feels that her definition is the one we all should use.) I claim, equally vehemently, that everyone has a right to define and name her- or himself, and if that means that there are four hundred million bisexuals with four hundred million definitions of the word, then we'll just have to live with that. (Naturally, I still think my definition is the one that makes the most sense.) I think I understand what she's getting at, and I think she understands what I'm getting at, too. But we have yet to come to an agreement.

This piece isn't about bisexuality, though. "Bisexual" is only one of the words that provokes this sort of conflict—the inability to agree on terminology, the angry, defensive vehemence that arguments over the terminology stir up. Other words leap to mind as well: racist, sexist, feminist; Christian, family, community; pornography, censorship; gay, lesbian, transsexual, transgender; dyke, faggot, queer, whore, slut, pervert, nigger (Christ, I can barely even bring myself to write that last one, much less say it). Forget about deciding whether or not we like the words, or whether we like the ideas and/or people they represent. We don't even know what they mean. And yet we use these words, and we use them the same way we use the rest of the language—as if we knew what the hell we were talking about.

So why is it so hard to come up with language that everyone agrees on? Why can't we agree that the definition of, say, "bisexual," will be such-and-such, and if there are people and ideas left out by that definition, simply agree to use a different word to describe those people and ideas? Nobody gets their knickers in a twist about what we mean by the word "blue." Nobody writes angry letters to the editor because the word "laundry" doesn't include bookshelves—or does include bed sheets. And the only people who have heated debates about the definition of the word "fish" are linguists and ichthyologists and people who are really stoned. (I have, in fact, had long weird discussions about what exactly constitutes a "salad," but these discussions certainly didn't have the life-or-death quality that the bi debates have had.)

Some words are loaded. And because they're loaded, coming up with definitions for them doesn't have the quasi-random quality that other words have—that sense that we call it this, but could easily have called it something else; that it doesn't really matter as long as we all call it the same thing, and if we find another thing that doesn't have a name, we'll just give it one. In the words that they'll probably carve on my gravestone—it's not that simple.

Loaded words are…well, *loaded.* They come with value and judgment attached, sometimes positive, sometimes negative and, very frequently, a muddled and weird combination of the two. At least some of the heated quality that these words carry has to do with the value attached to them. Pro-porn and anti-porn feminists attack one another by saying, "They're not really feminists"; progressive and fundamentalist Christians condemn one another by saying, "They're not truly Christian." Heavy players in the S/M community put down lighter players by saying, "Oh, she's just into bondage—she's not really a sadomasochist," and progressive gay activists dismiss conservative or apolitical people in the community by saying, "He may be homosexual, but I wouldn't call him gay." People place a high positive value on certain words; when they hear them used to describe people they ridicule or despise, the words themselves seems devalued.

Of course, a negative judgment can also contribute to making a word loaded. When a woman who sleeps with both women and men says she isn't bisexual because bisexuals are flaky and confused and don't care about anything but sex, her decision to call herself a lesbian instead is clearly influenced by—as well as contributing to—the negative weight ascribed to the word bisexual. If the word bisexual weren't so loaded, if it were a more neutral word, like Midwesterner or coffee drinker or brunette, she might be more likely to use it, and she might be more comfortable with her own behavior. For the record, I think she has the right to call herself a lesbian if she wants; like Miss Manners, I believe it is polite to address people in the way they wish to be addressed. But I suspect her choice of words is, at least partly, motivated by biphobia, by her belief that the word bisexual means "a bad person to be scorned and feared."

Even more complicated and heavily loaded are the words that carry both positive and negative weight. There are derogatory words, like queer and slut and whore and the notorious N word, that some people want to reclaim, even wear as a badge of honor, a Purple Heart for survivors of intolerance. There are words, like Christian or lesbian, that carry a different value judgment depending on who is speaking and who is listening. And there are words like sex and power and anger and pride, words that carry mixed judgments in themselves almost regardless of who says or hears them.

But the debates around these loaded words aren't just about whether or not we value the particular idea or type of person the words represent. I would argue that when we fight about the definitions of these words, often what we're actually fighting about is the hidden and unexamined concepts that underlie the language.

For example, when people debate the definition of the word bisexual, I believe that they are really debating other questions, questions that are complicated and messy and difficult to think about directly. Such as: Which is more important, who you have sex with or who you don't have sex with? Is sex more important than romance? Is sexual activity more important than sexual attraction? (Or the more universal version of that question: Is identity defined by feeling or behavior?) Is fantasy the same as desire? Is desire the same as intention? Is gender born, or learned, or both?

Look at the word "racist." There are huge, heated debates about it: whether it's possible for people of color to be racist, whether it's possible for white people not to be racist, whether certain opinions and beliefs and practices are racist by definition. When you boil them down, many of these arguments come down to a question of how the opponents define the word racism: as personal prejudice or as systematic oppression.

To say that a problem centers on a language barrier does not mean the problem is trivial. The differing definitions of the word "racist," for instance, point out seriously different ways of looking at the problem of racism. If you define racism as the systematic (if not always conscious) economic, political, social, cultural, and spiritual oppression of one race by another...well, that says something very different about you than if you define it simply as discrimination on the basis of race. It means you see the problem differently; it means you have a different sense of how important the problem is; and it probably means you see different responses and solutions.

There is often a circularity, a chicken-and-egg quality, to the definitions of loaded words. The way you perceive racism, for instance, will certainly affect the way you define the word; but the way you define the word will also affect how you perceive the concept. If you've always believed that racism is when one person treats another badly because of their skin color, you may have trouble even conceiving of a more widespread, insidious, class-oriented type of racism. But if you can't conceive of systematic racism, you probably won't see it when you look around you; and if you don't see any systematic racism around you, you'll probably keep on defining racism as personal prejudice....and merrily around the circle we go. Your definition of the word filters the way you see the world, and the way you see the world, filtered through your definitions, reinforces the way you use the word.

This circular nature of loaded language can have some very creepy,

Orwellian effects. A friend of mine was in a primarily gay/lesbian/bi/trans/queer/whatever-the-hell-you-want-to-call-it AIDS activism group that got into some very nasty bi wars. When the question of who got to define the word lesbian arose, one of the bi-phobic lesbian separatists came up with this solution: "The lesbians will define who is a lesbian." Now, in a purely semantic sense, this is a meaningless statement, even an absurd one, the sort of thing you might see in a lesbian version of *Alice in Wonderland.* But the sentence is not, in fact, meaningless. The implied meaning is crystal clear: "Women who do not and will not ever have sex with men will decide whether women who do or might have sex with men may be defined as lesbian." Or to put it another way, "The people who fit the most narrow definition of the word will decide whether or not the definition is to be expanded."

To me, this says a great deal, not only about how this woman defines the word lesbian, but also about how she perceives the community in general. It is a substantial dividing point in the gay/lesbian/bi/trans/queer/whatever community. Is it a public or private club? Does it include anyone who says s/he wants to join (and who pays their dues and brings cookies to the bake sale), or does it only include people who get recommended by current members?

These are not trivial, "how-many-angels-can-dance-on-the-head-of-a-pin" semantic debates. For one thing, the definition of a word determines who gets to be included in the activities of people defined by that word. If you're a transsexual woman attending a women's event, the definition of "woman" becomes much more than a question of semantics. It determines whether you'll be accepted and welcomed at the event or kicked in the ass and shown the door. Words have real-world consequences; it may seem like abstract quibbling to debate the definition of family, but when you look at adoption laws, and surrogate mothers, and kids being taken away from their queer parents, the question of who gets to be called family becomes very real indeed.

So when I hear the words, "The lesbians will define who is a lesbian," the meaning I hear is, "This is a private club. We have to maintain our high standards, or the place will be overrun by riffraff. Get a recommendation from two club members in good standing, and we will consider your request for admission at the next annual meeting." And that, folks, is not my vision of our community. My vision is that of a public club. If you say you want to join, if you show up and work and pay your dues, then you're a member, and you get to vote on the bylaws. That is my vision—and that is how I try to use the language.

When I look at the public vs. private club conflict, I begin to understand part of the reason these words are so loaded. The words aren't just about identity, or positive and negative value judgments. The words are about danger. The words a community uses to describe itself do more than just define the community; they define the perceived dangers to the community.

For instance, when anti-porn feminists say, "Susie Bright isn't really a feminist," or when pro-porn feminists say, "Andrea Dworkin isn't really a feminist," part of what they're arguing about is what they consider to be dangerous to women. Both groups might define a feminist as someone who sees women being injured by a sexist society and who fights to defend women from those injuries. But there are fierce arguments over what constitutes danger and threat and injury to women; degrading pornographic imagery that perpetuates objectification and violence against women, or fascistic and repressive censorship that silences the free expression of women's lives (to boil down just one of the debates to an oversimplified dogmatic summary). And when we argue over which of these dangers is most valid and most important and try to determine where and what we should be fighting, too often the discussion turns into a quarrel over who is or is not a feminist. The way the danger is perceived determines—at least partly—the way the word is defined.

And when lesbians argue over the inclusion or exclusion of bisexual women, the argument's focus, usually, is not on what would be good for the lesbian community, but on what might be harmful to it. The anti-bi lesbians fear pollution and betrayal, the pro-bi lesbians fear intolerance and McCarthyism. The bisexuals sit around wondering how the hell we got turned into the Frankenstein monster.

So which do you think is the greater danger? Impurity or elitism? Infiltration or divisiveness? Confusion or exclusion? The answers you give, I believe, will affect the way you define your community—and, therefore, yourself.

THE POLITIC IDENTITY:
QUESTIONING REPUTATIONS

Our adoption of queer identity may seem like a radical choice, an inborn and fundamental truth, or an uncovered secret (among countless other things). But once we adopt it, we become part of a larger culture with its own mores and worldview. We're challenged to match this image and identity as best we can, so that we can live within a supportive subculture. How much do we change to fit in, and how does that affect us? What do we embrace and what do we reject? Who does this leave out—when they're unwilling, or unable, to change—and why?

"Identity politics" implies that identities are fixed, nonproblematic, nonnegotiable—and that they come with built-in philosophies. If identity is multiple, slippery, contextualized, and negotiable, on what is our politics based? What do we really have in common with each other? This section introduces three writers who problematize identity in very different ways:

John Weir doubts the security of a queer identity until he's ventured down the path not taken. Katherine Raymond critiques a queer identity that enforces a dress code and chafes at the lack of congruence between the body and politics. D. Travers Scott rants about the narrowness of the trendy gay ghetto.

A critique of the assumptions that underlie identity politics wouldn't be complete without at least an acknowledgment (albeit not the in-depth investigation that these subjects deserve) that race, class, age, cultural difference, religious upbringing, and other differences intersect with our sex and gender identities, destabilizing the equation "identity=politics."

LIKE A VIRGIN

JOHN WEIR

It's Christmas Eve, and I'm in a wine bar in San Francisco trying to get laid. I flew here this morning. I ran out on my family, my friends, my holiday shopping, the leaky pipe in my bedroom, and all my past, present, and potential lovers in order to disappear into a new life on the Left Coast. I came here to be with a girl. Okay? I don't know why. Uranus was headed for my house of second chances and I figured it was time. That's one explanation. Here's another: I'm a thirty-six-year-old man, and I've never made love to a woman.

The bar's bright and empty. So far, the only person interested in me is my waiter. He's a Sagittarius, though, which means he's friends with everybody. I'm an Aquarius, which is why I don't mind asking questions. There's one, however, I've never asked until now. "Listen," I say, "do you know where I can meet some girls?" In the background, Annie Lennox is singing "Train in Vain." My waiter studies me a minute, stroking his goatee. "You're new here," he says finally, "aren't you?"

Well, yeah. The last time I flirted with a girl was my sophomore year of college, when I slid my hand up the back of a friend's sweater. I was borrowing her typewriter one night, and she put Joni Mitchell on the stereo and stretched across her bed. I'd been in this spot with women a few times before, and it always made me nervous. No matter how pretty the girl, I'd jump out of my head and watch myself caress her, thinking, "I should like this." My fear of not wanting it blew away any feelings I had about actually doing it. I'd shut down.

Guys always made me nervous, too. I'd think, "I shouldn't want this." I didn't know what I wanted; I only knew what I was told to want. Then shortly after college I met a guy who wanted me, and because it was such a relief to finally have sex with *some*one, and because I'd heard all my life that you had to be one or the other—gay or straight—I told everyone that I was gay.

As far as I know, I still am. But there are things you claim when you're twenty that don't seem so all-or-nothing fifteen years later. So radically self-defining. I ran away to California because that's where you go when the stories you tell yourself no longer apply. I was tired of being "gay." Tired of comparing myself to the simps and drag queens in TV shows and movies who are making homos "acceptable" to mainstream America. Tired of gay activists whining that homosexuality is an "orientation" and not a choice, as if to say that no sane person would ever choose it.

There seemed one sure way out of this: heterosexual sex. After all, I've always liked women better than men. They're smarter, stronger, and wiser, and besides, they call you back. The problem is I've never really, you know, *liked* them. Or rather, I'm terrified that I don't. This terror bugs me. I don't want to think of myself as a coward; I certainly don't want to think I'm gay because of what I'm afraid to do.

My waiter tells me I should check out Union Street, and a friend I call later says there's a Safeway in the Marina that's like a twenty-four-hour singles bar. I never get there. I don't go to the Buena Vista Café or the lobby of the Mark Hopkins Hotel or even one of the girlie showplaces in North Beach. Instead, I get the flu on Christmas Day and spend two weeks in a motel room taking echinacea through an eyedropper and watching "Peyton Place" over and over on AMC. Allison MacKenzie keeps trying to get Norman Page to kiss her. A friend calls in the middle of their embrace, and when I tell him what I'm doing in town, he laughs for five minutes. "What's so funny?" I say, watching Norman finally get aroused like I never did. "It's just," he says between gasps, "that you're so gay. I mean, you've said it in print. Who doesn't know?"

This is going to be harder than I thought.

Here's my fantasy: I'm at a party full of strangers. Lawyers, registered Republicans. Maybe it's a wine tasting, or a fundraiser for Bob Dole. I feel so out of place that I begin to enjoy it. I'm sipping an expensive Bordeaux when a fiercely smart woman with cheekbones you could cut your fingers on and arms like Angela Bassett's sits down next to me and notices my socks. She's from Harlem or Beverly Hills or both, and she's bitterly amusing. Before I know it, she's suggesting that we leave the party and go somewhere quiet. So I go. Who wouldn't? Hours later I wake in her bed, like a move hero after a discreet fadeout, his world forever changed....

You'll notice that I skip the sex and shift into third person. It's hard to stage a seduction, especially your own. However, I had some encouragement. A friend called up and offered herself. "Think about it and call me back," she said. "If you're really a straight guy, I won't hear from you." She didn't. I don't want a mercy fuck. I want to find out if my charm and beauty, and my, you know, masculine appeal are enough. I want to know what kind of straight guy I would be. But some of my straight pals said I was missing the point. "It doesn't matter what you're like," one guy said. "Straight, gay, whatever. None of that matters, 'cause John, I gotta tell you: not to be crass, but once you get it in there, man, it feels so good, you won't ever want to put it anywhere else."

I told him that sounded kind of like woman-as-receptacle. I asked if he'd ever had anal and/or oral sex, and if not, what was his standard of comparison. I said a lot of stuff which he and other guys shrugged off. They made pleas to my common sense, to the bottom line of pleasure, the glory that connects everyone with a penis and makes us all potential brothers. The joy of "getting in there." They didn't care if I liked women or not—they didn't necessarily like women themselves. Women were there for us to bond over.

My women friends were less thrilled. "I guess your next whim will be to sleep with a black person," one of them said accusingly. "I *hope* you use protection, at least," someone else said, at a friend's baby shower. Her idea, I guess, was that even though I'm HIV-negative, I'm still gay—that is, infectious by definition. But I get tested for HIV once a year and I know what I've done in bed, and who with, since I was twenty-four. I carry condoms even when I'm going out to the kitchen. How many straight guys, or girls, can say that?

My gay friends just laughed at me. Though a few of them, more feminist than any women I know, got huffy. Or righteous—they insisted I wouldn't be able to have sex with a woman, because sexual desire is a biological fact. In other words, people are gay or straight because they can't help it. Some gland controls desire. I don't believe that. I think desire is mysterious, but I don't think it's genetic. I'd like to think I'm gay because I want to be. The question is, How badly do I want to be straight?

It's Super Bowl Sunday. I'm back in New York and heading uptown at eleven o'clock at night for some action. I grab my Discman, toss Frank Sinatra's *Songs for Swinging Lovers!* in my knapsack, and get a cab. Ever since I decided to turn straight I've been drawn to Frank. It's a guy thing. I want to wear a cocked hat and a skinny tie and croon "Come Fly With Me" to a luscious babe. After all, I am a man of the '90s, bucking gender, class, race, history, personal opinion, and sexual desire. There's no telling who or what I am when I ask the cabbie to pull over in front of the Dublin House.

It's your basic bar, the kind of place you see in movies about midday drunks. Nicholas Cage could die here. Or he could just hang out, like the four women at the end of the bar under the twenty-inch television screen. When I ask the bartender, Mike, for a Rolling Rock, the girl closest to me says, "Bass." She's lounging on a barstool, in a black pullover and black stretch pants, and she's got a lot of brown hair spilling sweetly over her shoulders. But her voice stings like rye. "Get the Bass," she repeats, lighting a Dunhill. It's too late. Mike delivers my Rock, and she turns back to her three buddies. I sip the wrong drink, feeling grateful and rejected at once. She noticed me! Too bad that what she noticed was my bad taste in beer. Wait until she finds out I suck dick.

Unless she already knows. Because, as far as I can tell, I'm queer as a three-dollar bill. Or rather, queer as a Lincoln penny, because you never see a three-dollar bill, whereas my queerness is something everybody sees. It always has been. People have been calling me a fag since I was seven years old, long before I had a conscious sexual feeling for anyone. Something about my voice, my body, my gestures, my personality gave me away. I haven't trusted myself since.

So when one of the Bass woman's friends makes a pass at me, I'm completely surprised. "Sorry," she says, in a British accent, "but you're not leaving town, are you?" The others giggle.

"You're looking for a sublet?" I say, trying to be charming. "Or do you *want* me to leave town?"

"Oh, it's a rather long story."

I say, "I've got time," which strikes me as unbearably smooth.

The woman sitting next to her suddenly introduces everybody. Her name's Denise, she says, grinning unsurely. The Bass woman is Tina, the English girl is Blair, and the willowy athletic-looking girl who just ran off to the bathroom is Bob. Anyway, that's what Denise tells me.

"So, Denise," I say, enjoying her, "why does Blair want me to leave town?"

"*I'll* tell him," Blair says. She's wearing overalls and looks like the farm girl the hero doesn't marry in a D.H. Lawrence novel. "It's simple enough," she says. "The last two men I had sex with—well, they both left town shortly after."

"Oh," I say.

Denise blushes, like she wants me to know she's less brash than Blair. Then Bob comes back, looking like Mariel Hemingway in Personal Best.

"Hi, Bob," I say.

She says, "I'm sorry?" Another British accent.

"My brother's name is Bob," I say.

She looks at Denise. "I'm Emma."

"That's my brother's middle name," I say, more for Denise than for Bob. Denise and I are sharing a joke. I'm liking her. She's shy but she's playful.

"Don't you have a girlfriend?" Denise asks. She has a lopsided smile and messy hair, which makes me feel safe.

"No, in fact, I don't."

Tina scoffs. "There're only four reasons for that," she says, counting them out on her fingers. "One: You can't commit. Two: You've been badly burned. Three: You're a mama's boy. Or four: You're gay."

"Gosh," I say coyly. "Two out of four."

"You've been burned!" Denise says, helpfully. "And what else?"

"Well," I say, "I'm not a mama's boy."

"You don't look like the kind of guy who can't commit," Denise says, hopefully. I'm trying to decide if I think she's sexy.

"I didn't say I couldn't commit."

"Then you're gay," Tina says, not trusting me.

"Bob," I say, "help me out here."

Bob's twenty-three. She's a nanny for two small children and plays electric guitar. She knows the answers to many things. "Here it is, then," she says. "You take a girl to see *Bed of Roses*, okay? You know that movie? If you watch it with a girl, then buy her flowers, you'll be right in there."

"You'll get laid easy," Blair agrees.

"He's not that kind of guy," Denise says. "Are you?" She's got that edgy look which means she wants to go past flirting, maybe. She likes me. I like her, too. I don't know what to do: ask for her number, offer mine? I'm not thinking about sex, just conversation, alone. Then Tina and Bob leave, and Blair goes to the bathroom, and I get the chance.

"So I guess you have a boyfriend, right?" I say.

She moves closer. She's got brown eyes and a pensive smile, as if she were framing a question I won't know how to answer.

"No, I don't," she says simply.

"Oh," I say, and I get that old familiar nervous feeling. We talk for a while before Blair comes back, and there's a moment when I know it's my turn to say, "Wanna trade numbers?" I almost do—but I don't. She brushes her hair back uncertainly, then stretches her hand across the bar and we touch. Then I say good-night.

I never believe straight guys when they say they can't imagine sex with a man. "You're afraid you'll like it," I tell them, not admitting I'm afraid, too. I'm afraid I won't like what I'm supposed to like. And then I'll know for sure I'm not a man.

This issue of what it means to be a man comes up with my friend Nick, a straight guy who wants to help me get laid. We go out drinking one night with his friend Hector, and they try to set me up with the cocktail waitress. "Would you sleep with a gay guy who's never had sex with a girl before, but he's curious?" Hector asks.

"Sure," she says. "Are you ordering?"

"There you go," Nick says. "You're in there."

"She just wants a tip," I say, and I go to the men's room. When I come back, Nick and Hector are talking about fistfights.

"I was at a party last week," Hector says, "and I fought with this guy. It was like, he punched me in the face, I punched him in the face, he punched me, I punched him." He leans forward and throws out his fists, pow-pow-pow-pow. "And if I see that guy on the street, man, I'll buy him a drink. It was like a total rush, you know?"

Hey, that sounds familiar: pow, pow, pow, pow, get in there fast, get out faster, then go have a drink.

"You guys are such fags," I want to say, but remembering Hector's fists, I don't.

Later that week, I go out with my friend Steve and his buddy Tim. Steve's twenty-one and Tim's twenty-four and they're both cute and sexy. They take me to Bob, a downtown club the size of my living room. It's so crowded it takes ten minutes to cross the floor. We order Rocks. We're not trying to impress anybody. Anyway, it's not a club where you have to work hard, or even move, to be pressed up against someone exciting.

I turn to my left and bump into a girl. I say, "Pardon me for happening in three dimensions." She says, "Yes, yes, yes, yes, yes." She's this total Molly Bloom. "Yes, what?" I say. "Yes whatever," she says. I ask her name. She says, "Safari." I say, "No kidding?" "Oh, yes," she says. "Oh, yes, yes, yes, yes, yes."

"Hey guys," I say, handing her over, which seems to be what she wants, "this is Safari." Steve says, "No shit." Safari says, "So. So, so, so." She's cute and eager—Natalie Portman, only legal—and she's got a friend named Anne, who's tall and reluctant, the kind of girl who leaves her pals at home when she's going downtown. She hates us, and Safari knows it. But they're some kind of Jekyll-and-Hyde combo, because the more Anne hates us, the more Safari flirts, and it makes them both happy.

"How wild is that?" Steve says. I leave him and Tim to flirt with Anne and Safari, and squeeze across the floor. The room's layered like the core of the earth, with a molten center where people are dancing. Heads and hands and dreadlocks go up in the air, and sunglasses catch the light. Surrounding this are black boys standing still and white girls moving slowly toward them. The crowd's more mixed and way more fun than in any gay bar. I didn't know straight people got so raw. I'm spun by centrifugal force into a circle of three Cuban girls from Miami who are clutching Cuba Libres and smoking cigarettes and bumping their hips at anybody passing by.

"*Hola, amigas,*" I say, and thank god they laugh. One of them, Claudia, takes my hand and says, "Dance with me." I say, "Do women do this? Just, like, dance with guys?" And Claudia says, "Oh, baby, hush your mouth." She's small and young and sassy, and she twirls me into the middle of the circle like I'm this giant goat boy writhing among the maenads.

She pulls me close, against her breasts, which are as lovely as Patricia Arquette's. I'm thinking, "She's drunk, she's nineteen. How is going home with a smashed kid I'll never see again any different from being a gay man?"

Then Steve shows up. He grabs my arm and says, "Safari's being weird, let's go." And before I have a chance to get nervous about Claudia, we leave.

If I weren't so nervous about girls, I'd be dating Denise right now. Or avoiding Claudia's calls. Or pining over that cocktail waitress. Instead, I'm pining over the cute straight guys who take me drinking. They listen to my stories about girls coming on to me and wonder what I'm waiting for. I'm waiting for it to feel right. Finally, I say to hell with being a nice boy. To hell with romance. I toss out Frank Sinatra and put on the Buzzcocks, "Orgasm Addict," and decide to take my emotions out of it. I decide to pay for sex. First I call my buddy Nick.

"Hey," I say, "wanna have sex with me?"

"That's unlikely," he says.

"Because I'm going to a prostitute. I figure if I pay someone to sleep with me, it'll be her job not to care if I don't want to do it. I mean, I don't want to hurt anyone's feelings."

"Oh, man."

"And I was hoping you'd come along and, you know, encourage me. Slap me on the back."

"Do I get a girl, too?"

"Sure."

"Are you gonna pay?"

"Sure."

"Cool," Nick says, and a week later we're sitting down with a bottle of scotch, a pack of Marlboros, a cordless phone, and the classified pages from the back of a magazine, picking out brothels. I make Nick do the calling. He's reliably male, pulling on a cigarette and taking hits on his scotch. "Let's try this place," he says. "It's called Blossom Time. Well, isn't that literary?" He hands me the phone and says, "Be a man." Then he goes in the kitchen and pours us both another scotch.

"What's the deal?" he says, back with our drinks. He's twenty-two, but compared to me he's a man of the world. At least with women. He's small and tightly wired, aimed at life like a missile. He calls his dick the Star Destroyer.

"It's a metaphor," he says.

"I get it," I say, thinking, "Hey, maybe that's what I've been missing. A nickname for my penis."

There are three girls at Blossom Time, each $160 an hour plus tip, which is half what some places charge. We go out for breath mints, then get a cab across town.

The place turns out to be a two-bedroom apartment in a tenement building above a Greek restaurant. There's a woman on a couch watching TV in an old shirt, a guy in jeans hanging out in the kitchen, and a woman with bleached hair who leads us to a small room with a TV set and a double bed. "You guys want drinks?" she says. Nick says we brought our own, and she goes for cups and ice. I sit on the bed. "Yo, little buddy," I say to Nick, dudelike.

"What are we, on 'Gilligan's Island'?"

The TV's tuned to Howard Stern, whose guest is Tom Jones. Tom's singing Prince's "Kiss" when the door opens a peekaboo width and there's a black woman in a white minidress who says, "I'm Heather."

"Hey now," Nick says. Heather's gone. The second woman opens the door more shyly. She's a white girl, blond, pretty, but she's no Heather. When she leaves, the woman comes back with our drinks.

"Where's the third girl?" Nick says.

"She's out on a call," the woman says. "You guys want the room together?"

"Hell no," Nick says.

"Okay, then which girl do you want?" the woman asks me, and I think, If I knew how to answer that question, my whole life would be different.

"He wants Heather," Nick says, nodding and smiling. I get sent to the other room, which is big enough for a bed and another TV set. I feel weird leaving Nick, but that's what guys do. Heather comes in and says,

"You get comfortable as the day you were born." Then she leaves. I sip my scotch, even though I've already had too much. I take off my shoes and socks, roll my watch in my socks, and stuff them inside one of my shoes. There's a mirror at the head of the bed and a painting high up on the wall. When Heather comes back, I ask her what her sign is.

"Why do you want to know?" she says. She's got long black hair, down to her butt. The TV gets radio reception, and she flips through salsa and disco and "Losing My Religion" until she finds some nice, bland jazz. Now I'm in my shorts and a muscle T-shirt, without the muscles. "Too many Mounds bars," I say apologetically, patting my stomach, and she says, "You taking those off? My birthday's in July."

"You're a Cancer," I say. "Secretive and maternal. As if there's a difference. That's a joke," I say, and she says, "Uh huh," and she's naked, and then so am I. She's beautiful. I feel weird saying that, because she's twenty and black and I'm older and white, and she's a prostitute and I'm paying her. But it's hard to debate racial and sexual politics when you're buck naked in a bedroom with a woman who's Halle Berry crossed with Madonna, and your basic worry is getting it up.

"You're not ready yet," she says, and I laugh too loud. I don't mention I'm gay; she doesn't ask. I just say, "I've never done this before," feeling ashamed and guilty at once. Suddenly I understand Catholicism. "I mean, pay for sex." She says "Uh huh" again, not caring. She doesn't need me. She's got such an amazing body, it doesn't even have to be lit right to look good. Her stomach's flat and her breasts are lovely and smallish and high and she has an alert, caustic, tender, self-confident grace, and a ring in her navel. I say, "You should be a movie star," and she laughs and says, "Take another sip of your drink." Then I roll on my stomach and she massages my back.

"Relaxed?" she says, and I say, "Too relaxed," and I roll on my side and point down and say helplessly, "Maybe some oil on that?" I don't know what to call it. Not Star Destroyer. Anyway, it doesn't matter because the oil works, and she says, "Lick my titties," and I think, "Oh, boy, now we're getting somewhere."

There's no time for nervousness, because suddenly I'm touching her. I've got my arms around her and my hand is in the curve of her back and she's small but I feel smaller, cradled, nursing. I'm cuddled against her and her head's tipped back and it's fine. That's all. I think, "Wow, she's lovely." I think, "Wow, I wish I had her abs." It'd be nice to kiss her, but she won't kiss. I've had this kind of sex before with guys, sex someone doesn't especially want, sex where body parts are offered one at a time and in order, with some crucial steps left out. I like to kiss. But that's not part of the agreement. I guess it doesn't matter, because if she were a man and he were this sexy, I wouldn't miss the kissing. If she were a man it would feel different, not because of her or him, but because of me. I like her body. I'm grateful for her attitude, aloof but friendly. She talks dirt, which is the one thing I don't like, but when she says, "Eat my pussy," I'm like, Well, how else would you ask someone to do that? So I do it. I decide I'm not going to get HIV from a woman, which is crazy, I know. I'd never be so carefree with a guy. Now I know how straight men who sometimes have sex with other men do it without worrying about AIDS—they think, Hey, I'm not in this risk group. I'm in another risk group. So this is safe. That's what I tell myself, foolishly. I'm out of my category, so the rules don't apply.

Anyway, it's what I'm most curious about. Her vagina. I know how touching feels, and I know how penetration feels, and I know what orgasms are like to have and to watch, but I don't know anything about anyone's pussy. Okay? I've listened to grown men, gay and straight, say things like it's smelly, it's bottomless, it's devouring; or it's mystic, it's divine, it's nirvana. I've got fantasies that when I touch it with my tongue I'll be transformed. I'll want to say "Mother." I'll want to say "God." I'll want to say "I finally belong." What happens instead is I put my nose in Heather's vagina, and she's getting paid, and I'm gay, and she says, "Oh, baby, you're so good."

I laugh. She laughs. She says, "What the hell?" I say, "Wow, it's totally cool." Because it is. I'm like, Go, girl, there's your pussy. Nothing nasty or godly about it. It's just, you know, her genitalia. Genitals are wacky, admit it. I mean, explain a penis. I'm delighted to find out that she's like me—she's got strange body parts that feel good in somebody's mouth. It's a relief. I'm happy that women can be undignified, too. I'm happy that we're all still little kids wanting our fingers in out-of-sight places. I'm happy to finish my hour doing this to her. The only thing I'm not is aroused.

It's like I'm idling in neutral. I like the fantasy that I'm giving her pleasure, and I'm hard, but I'm not turned on. Her body's not so different from a man's: There are all the same limbs, the shoulders, the hips and ass, and the nutty, willful private parts. What she doesn't have is my longing. I don't know what desire is, but I'm sure it's not physical. What I feel with men is a lack, a tightness, an anxiety, a yearning to get something back that I lost. I call that yearning, you know, chest hair. Or the smell of shaving cream. Or a tone of voice. There's nothing about Heather's body that makes me achy or dizzy. There's no charge.

So when she wants me inside of her, I'm like, Sure, I'll do that. She gets a condom on me and our date is over. I want to say right here, in spite of anything I've ever said about safe sex and men's responsibility for birth control, that condoms are the worst thing in the world. I hate them, I can't feel anything through them, I wish they were never invented. I'd rather not have intercourse at all. What's the big deal about screwing somebody—anybody—anyway? It doesn't make me feel, whatever...manly, indispensable, pink with pleasure. But all the straight guys and a lot of the gay ones I know are all hung up on it, as though they all read The Sun Also Rises when they were twelve and never got over how Jake Barnes couldn't fuck because his dick got mangled in the war. Didn't anybody ever mention oral sex to Ernest Hemingway?

I'm making excuses. Here's what happened: I stayed inside her a couple minutes. Then I wanted to change positions, and that was that. I lost it. I never came. I didn't want to, really, and she didn't care. She got up off the bed and went for baby wipes, and I said, "That's it?" and she said, "That's it," and then she told me that she works for an airline in her spare time. "Nobody with any brains works full-time for an airline," she said.

And then she's gone, and I'm back in the living room with Nick, who finished before I did. "I want some fries, Nick, let's get some fries," I say, "and a cigarette, I want to smoke a cigarette," and he says, "Did you get in there?" and I say, "For a minute, but we switched positions and I lost it," and he claps me on the back and says, "Hey, of course, that's understandable, changing positions, that's always a risk, sure, that's happened to me. I should have told you before, pick a position and stick to it—hey now, but you got in there."

I smoke his cigarette. We walk to an outdoor café. I'm buying. He has a burger and tells me about his girl, who wasn't much fun. Then he flirts with the waitress. She's a Taurus. I order fries. Nick's fries have cheese and I share them. I love Nick. He's swell. I tell him about going down on Heather, and he praises me again. "More fries for you," he says, like that's my reward.

And it is. I went out two months ago to find a woman and ended up here, at a sidewalk café, eating some guy's cheese fries and watching him be cute for a girl. It's twice as exciting as Heather's body. Desire is what you don't have. It's not women I want. I don't even really want men. What I want is that unquestioned ease in the world, like Nick flirting with the waitress without caring about his awkwardness or realizing his grace. I want a woman so I can see myself, even briefly, even just in Nick's eyes, as a man.

CONFESSIONS OF A SECOND-GENERATION... DYKE?:
REFLECTIONS ON SEXUAL NON-IDENTITY

KATHERINE RAYMOND

It's hard enough to be "queer" (or whatever) in a heterosexist, homophobic society, and to feel the pressure of constantly asserting your "sexuality," as a defined entity, in a society where straightness, as the unmasked term, is assumed until proven otherwise. It's hard enough to be unsure what exactly this monolithic "sexual identity" of yours is, and constantly wonder whether it makes sense to "out" yourself, again and again in an endless stream of new situations, when it's not even clear exactly what it is you're "outing," or whether you have a right to claim membership in the world of queerness. It's bad enough feeling like you're living a lie if you allow straight people to assume you're totally straight and gay people to assume you're totally gay. But having to think about all this when you're not even getting laid has to be the most depressing thing of all.

I've been with men and I've been with women. Right now I'm not with anyone. I hate the word "bisexual" for a litany of reasons, not least because it seems to imply that I should feel twice as undesirable as anybody else when I'm not in a relationship. And while in theory I would like to be open to being with men or with women, in practice it seems almost impossible to be in a lesbian relationship without making an exclusive commitment to women, or vice versa.

I don't look like a lesbian. Maybe this is a politically-incorrect statement to make, but it is an honest one. It seems to me that the more emphasis queer theory and politics place on the endless multiplicity of sexual personae, and the more well-meaning postmodernists problematize what exactly a gay man, lesbian, or bisexual "is," the easier it gets to describe what one looks like. At least in New York City, where I live, there is a clearly-defined gay community with very explicit visual cues declaring one's inclusion or exclusion. In college I called them the "short-hair fascists." I just don't look good with short hair (my face is very round), and from the age of six I rebelled against my then-crunchy feminist mom by preferring frilly dresses and Mary Janes to cords and sensible shoes. (I've since come around to cords, but I bought my last pair of shoes solely to match my nails.) And for all the recent spate of "butch/femme" theory that attempts to reclaim the femme as an integral component of butch/femme duality, the fact remains that if I try to make flirtatious eye contact with a butch woman on the street, she looks right through me— or worse, averts her eyes with a pained look that suggests thoughts along the lines of, Why is that straight girl staring at me?

Lately in the queer movement there's been an all-too-facile equation of "sexuality" and "identity," in which one's personal style, political affiliations, work, and—for lack of a better word—"lifestyle" are organized around one's queer sexuality. It's understandable, especially in a place like New York where so many diverse (but necessarily tolerant) groups of people are gathered, that queer men and women would develop a visual signifying system to assert queer presence without being obligated to "come out" in every new social context. As someone who never gets visually "pegged" as gay, I know that it can be awkward at best and painful at worst when people assume you're exclusively heterosexual. But for me, assuming a queer style just isn't a reflection of who I am.

Many people I know count queerness as a definitive part of their individual identities. For those who grew up in heterosexual families, coming out must have been a declaration on many levels of having found oneself, reconciled with one's true identity. Queerness did not play such a role in my formative identity, because I grew up with a lesbian mom.

As a child growing up in a predominantly Irish Catholic suburb of Boston, I internalized a lot of the homophobia of the community—as

well as feeling uncomfortable with my mother's complete openness about
her sexuality—and it took a while for me to feel okay about the fact that
I didn't have a "normal" family. In high school, my form of subconscious
rebellion was sleeping with boys and being as reactionary as I possibly
could; for me, individuating from my mother meant being completely
antifeminist. (Perhaps not coincidentally, I was at that time disgusted by
my own body, not to mention by the idea of lesbian sex.) But I gradually came to terms with my mom's (and my own) sexuality, aided in large
part by my decision to go to college in New York City, a decidedly more
"progressive" environment than Boston. My growing acceptance of and
pride in my mom's identity, as an outspoken feminist and activist as well
as a lesbian, crystallized when I met and became friends with several
women my age who were going through the coming-out process. When
they looked to my mother as a heartening example of a lesbian with a
successful career and a family, I appreciated for the first time what it
meant to have grown up with a role model who rejected traditional
patriarchal values.

By my senior year of college, I was born again as a lesbian feminist, I
saw the error of my earlier ways and adopted "girl power | girl love=rev-
olution" as my mantra. In college, an isolated community in itself, the
idea of existing within a lesbian community made sense to me; it was a
source of support, a framework within which to organize my identity.
The first time I fooled around with a girl, we joked to each other that
we could now go get our membership cards. Because I was already existing within a self-contained community on the college campus, this elitism, and the apparent need to prove oneself in terms of physical appearance or sexual contact in order to gain inclusion in this group, didn't
bother me. College life, with its variety of classes and activities, provided
so many opportunities to meet and get to know people within the course
of an average day, that I was able to mark myself as a member of a queer
community based on who I knew, not what I looked like.

But after I graduated into the "real world" (such as it is, in New York) and got a job that took up most of my time and energy, I realized that it wasn't possible to exist within a lesbian community—within a lesbian identity—unless I adopted a physical style that didn't in any way reflect me personally and organized my social life specifically around meeting and dating lesbians. Off campus, it simply wasn't that easy to let my life, my identity, revolve around sexuality in that way.

As a "twentysomething" person living in New York City, I often feel like life among my peers revolves around going to work, getting off work, and going out drinking. I don't have the time, energy or money to go to bars, gay or straight, all the time; nor do I really envision myself seeking and finding a meaningful relationship in one. There are other things I want to (and, financially speaking, have to) do with my time and for myself besides cruise for a woman or a man.

It's true that going out to bars is not the only mode of "queer lifestyle" available to me in New York, though it sometimes seems that way. I've considered becoming more involved in politics aside from my writing. But beyond the occasional Pride march, political rallies and meetings aren't really my scene—maybe it's because of all the demonstrations my mom dragged me to when I was a kid. I'm just not the activist type, so involving myself in queer political groups would feel to me like a forced way to "meet people" and integrate a queer identity into my life. And given that I work full time, with freelance work on the side, investing time and energy into a political organization—much less doing so largely to "meet chicks"—would feel like more of a forced attempt to integrate "queerness" into my "lifestyle" than a genuine commitment to queer causes.

For perhaps the first time in my life, I'm beginning to value myself based on factors other than whether or not I'm in a relationship. While it would be nice to have someone special in my life, I don't think it would be healthy for me to put too much energy into searching for that someone. I'm young, and there are other things I want to do with my life. I feel like love will find me when it's meant to. But in the world of compulsory heterosexuality, this attitude is tantamount to consigning myself to heterosexuality by default.

I'm definitely very attracted to boys, but I feel almost guilty about that fact, because it seems obvious that if I wait for a relationship to find me, that relationship is likely to be a straight one. Practically speaking, it's difficult to have a sexuality other than the default one without organizing your life around it. Straight people seem able to fit sexual relationships into their lives without major conflict; sexuality, while part of everyone's life, isn't a definitive factor in one's "lifestyle." Straights have the privilege of pursuing their own interests and activities while keeping an eye out for romantic prospects. But in a heterosexist, homophobic society, non-straight people can't just assume that people they find attractive are necessarily romantic prospects; a romantic proposition or flirtation with someone of the same sex is a risky endeavor.

This taboo on same-sex flirtation derives from and enforces compulsory heterosexuality. Even though I find myself more drawn of late to boys, in terms of physical attractions, fantasies, and desires, it seems hypocritical of me to slip back into overdetermined straightness as the path of least social resistance, after all my idealistic college dreams of girl love. Yet at the same time, I resent the fact that I can't just "keep my options open" in terms of the romantic and sexual routes available to me. "Queerness" seems to have taken on so many levels of social and political significance beyond and outside sexuality that it goes beyond mere sexual preference. "Queerness" is a state you either exist in all the time or don't exist in at all.

My mom has always spoken contemptuously of bisexuals as fair-weather friends to the gay community, people who ditched their politics when in a straight relationship. I certainly saw plenty of this variety of boy-crazy bisexual women in college (a friend referred to one as "Dyke Lite"), and vowed to myself that I would never sell out like that. I strongly believed, and still do, that I could never just turn my back on queer politics, even if I'm involved primarily through writing rather than activism.

After all, growing up with my mom, I experienced homophobia long before I even had a formed sexuality, and I could never forget that experience. In retrospect, it showed me that homophobia is about blind hatred, and affects people regardless of whom they do or don't sleep with. I believe that it benefits everyone to fight homophobia, and that I can and should be committed to doing so in whatever way I can, regardless of my personal sexual proclivities and activities.

I also see now that my mom's biphobia is largely based on the fact that she herself is on some level attracted to men as well as women. Her choice to be a lesbian is based on a political commitment; she resents those women who don't make that commitment, and want to have it both ways by claiming "marginalized" status yet enjoying heterosexual privilege. I respect my mother's putting herself on the line by coming out in the context of a much more homophobic community than the one in here in New York in the late '90s, and I understand her expecting fellow "queers" to remain committed to queer politics regardless of their sexual partners. But I still don't know how it would be possible for me to be a part of the queer community while in a relationship with a man—or even while not in a relationship with a woman, as I am now. I feel that there's some kind of burden of proof on me, as someone who claims membership in a queer community, to be a lesbian, or at least rack up enough "lesbian points" to feel politically safe being with a man without being perceived as a traitor. Inasmuch as my sexuality has evolved over time along with my political beliefs, I can understand the lesbian community's tendency to hold people politically responsible for their sexual desires and activities. Yet at any given moment, I experience attraction as a physical, possibly emotional, but in no way as a political feeling.

In short, sexuality seems to me to be about the body—whether in terms of appearance or of sex—which is probably as it should be. But when sexuality has become equivalent to "identity," it seems impossible to exist outside these rigid categories, where there's no such thing as being open to queer sexuality without organizing an identity around it, and no such thing as getting to have queer sex without first establishing and defining this identity.

Some people think that any sex can be "queer" sex if the partners bring a "queer" sensibility to the act; for example, a woman fisting a man up the ass isn't exactly "straight" sex. This is one of those nice postmodern concepts which suggests infinite subversive meaning in any text (including the body), depending on who is doing the suggesting. But how much can any given sex act really signify, or really subvert?

It's certainly true that the personal is political, in the sense that one's identity, even in its most "intimate" components, is informed by a larger sociopolitical context. Yet the idea that individual sex acts will, over time, somehow permeate and alter the collective social consciousness seems a bit suspect to me. The causal gaps between sex acts and political theory, to say nothing of those between theory and political practice, are vast and indefinable. It's difficult to make the argument that one female fist inserted into one male ass—or, for that matter, dozens or even hundreds of fists inserted into as many asses—can really make a difference for, say, lesbian mothers fighting for custody of their children. It's true that my mom being queer made me more aware of the existence of queer sexuality and more open to the possibility of being queer myself. But does my not having sex with twice as many people really make the world a better place?

In my embittered, not-getting-any state, I have come to wonder whether sex isn't a purely selfish act. Are queers and straights and everyone in between kidding themselves if they really think what they do or don't do in bed—or the complex theoretical essays they write about what they do in bed—are directly or indirectly going to change society? Lately I'm the only one in my bed, and while I've read articles that debate the "queerness," or the subversiveness, of masturbation, I have trouble believing that what I do quietly behind closed doors affects anybody but myself. As queer identity—and, conversely, homophobia—are often based in large part on factors other than what people actually do in bed, the solitary activity of masturbation seems to have little power to signify in social or political realms.

This disjuncture between what I actually am or identify as, inasmuch as I even know myself, and how that self is received or perceived by my social context, has informed my own confused sense of my identity as well as of identity politics in general. Growing up relatively dark-skinned in the predominantly Irish town of Quincy, Massachusetts, I got called "spic" as I walked down the streets of my neighborhood. I happen not to be Hispanic (my family is Assyrian-American, an ethnicity for which few personalized slurs exist), and at the time I don't think I knew what the word meant, but the hatred in that name-calling was not lost on me. If anything, there was a particular kind of insult-added-to-injury in the complete irrelevance of this taunting to who I was in any sense beyond the simple fact that I was "different." A few years later, when my mom came out, I would cringe inwardly whenever kids shouted "fag" and "lezzie" at each other on the playground. The experience was a similar awareness of hatred that implicated me but was fundamentally not about me. The prejudices and stereotypes that hurt me were not only ignorant and unjust, they were irrelevant to any active sense of identity I had then developed.

Since my sexuality has evolved to include attraction to both women and men, I've experienced a similar sense of awkward disjuncture in the presence of straight acquaintances who use "queer" as a pejorative term, as well as with lesbian friends who refer to straight women with barely-veiled contempt. In each of these situations I find myself wondering: Who do I side with? Who do I speak for? Who is it my place to defend? Who is it my place to criticize? If I voice my objections, will I actually succeed in changing anyone's opinions, or only in alienating myself?

I don't mean to say that I think homophobia was or is not my problem. Like it or not, it is my problem. It hurt a lot, and still does whenever I encounter it. It's just that homophobia—and the queer subculture's occasional reaction of defensive elitism—is by definition ignorant, and as such has nothing to do with who I really am, or who any queer (or straight) person really is.

That's why I resent the implicit imperative to organize one's identity around queerness, to walk down the street wrapped in a mantle of "queerness" based on the way one is physically marked. I would like to fight for gay rights regardless of whom I have sex with, or don't. I would like to desire, to fantasize, without censoring myself based on the political implications of thoughts no one else will ever hear. I don't want to feel guilty for not getting any. I want to be a sexual being without defining myself solely or even primarily on the basis of my sexuality.

LE FREAK, C'EST CHIC! LE FAG, QUELLE DRAG!:
CELEBRATING THE COLLAPSE OF HOMOSEXUAL IDENTITY

D. TRAVERS SCOTT

My boyfriend and I just moved to the gay ghetto. I've never really lived in the gay ghetto before. A brief stint near Chicago's Boystown was spent in a mouse-infested basement apartment whose floor gave way from the wall, whose toilet never worked, and whose front window framed hookers' stilettos. There I dated two straight men and had more sexual incidents with women than fags. So, despite my physical proximity to the Pride Parade route, the ubiquitous Curl Up & Dye salon, kitchen ceramics boutique, and several queer commodity outlets, I wasn't really living the gay lifestyle.

I am now.

My boyfriend and I fell into jobs in a new city, returning to full-time work after years of freelancing. As we prepared to move, we decided we were fed up with low-rent artists' dives in obscure neighborhoods where we couldn't get pizza delivered. We wanted some convenience. So we got an overpriced apartment in Seattle's queer/boho Capitol Hill, within quick walking distance to our jobs, plus bookstores, bars, coffee shops, etc. It's nice having neighbors who will look us in the eyes. It's nice not turning off the Christopher Rage video when the building manager drops by. It's nice getting sucked off in the laundry room.

Yes, sex is *very* convenient here. In addition to my dear boyfriend, there's jerk-offs at the YMCA, a dozen bars within arm's length, the ceaselessly cruisey Broadway Ave ("I'm just out to buy toilet paper, okay?! I'm *really* not cruising!"), the adult theater, the johns at the parks, sex clubs A, B or C (D is downtown, and that's *such a hike*), and the afore-mentioned friendly neighbors.

It's also easy to shop here. Proudly-queer clothes, videos, churches, snacks, meals, coffee, books, mags, and music glare from every shop window, should the preponderance of lust outlets not serve as reminder enough of one's faggottry. Homo propaganda is everywhere, in the form of banners, badges, and posters, like some rainbowed *1984*. And it's all for sale. You have an endless supply of ready-made identity signifiers: all the mass-pro-duced knick-knacks to show off and celebrate your oh-so-uniquely-*you* Queer Identity. Camp/retro/kitsch fashions and furnishings abound, and Urban Outfitters is so much more convenient (and smells better) than trudging through Goodwill. *Genre* and *Out* are so kind as to provide handy shopping guides so we don't have to search boutique after bou-tique to find faux antique photo frames, porno screen savers, and rain-bow dildo electric toothbrushes. For the first time since I was sixteen, I received a copy of *International Male* in the mail addressed to me, and I didn't even have to order it. It must automatically come to every address in this zip code, like those coupon packs.

I scraped off the mailing label and took it straight to the recycling before the neighbors could see.

Don't get me wrong, I'm not totally bashing queer neighborhoods. I realize it's a luxury that I even have one to grouse about. I've always said I thought separatism and strength in numbers were good when you needed them. It's a healing and strengthening phase. Some of the rural kids who move here probably desperately need this validation and sup-port. But achieving a well-accessorized Queer Identity is only a phase, not a destination, end product, or utopia, and it's time we stop treating it as such. Urban gay ghettos may be really comfy and safe little scenes but they are part of a decadent, mannerist, final phase before the movement shifts into something else entirely.

It's already happening. The constant pride, boasting, and reaffirming of

Queer Identity all are beginning to seem childishly obvious. You're here, you're queer, we're over it. When even the faggot bible *Genre* runs an article titled "We're So Over the Rainbow," you know something's up. The parades have gone from being revolutionary to boring as shit. Besides, the names are too long: the Gay, Lesbian, Bisexual, Transgendered & Friends Show does not roll trippingly off the tongue. (Don't even try to pull that "lesbigay" shit, our little Esperanto that some well-intentioned fool came up with. And "queer" almost immediately came to mean "saucy fags and dykes," not the radically-sexualized boundary-breaking coalition it was first advertised to be, or we'd have a hell of lot more heterosexual "queers" in our parades.)

But beyond semantic bitching, there are larger issues at stake. All this Pride and Identity and Culture and Community, frankly, get in the way. They're awkward, clunky albatrosses, limiting concepts which simply don't work anymore. Witness gay men and lesbians coming out of the closet—they're admitting that they've fallen in love with and married heterosexuals of the opposite sex. And many were not bisexuals to begin with. It could happen to even the most devout Kinsey Six: if your hormones were powerful enough to make you break with the norms of a heterosexual society, do you honestly think you could never fall for a person of the opposite sex? To paraphrase Tennessee Williams, "a line is straight, a road may be straight, but the heart curves and curves." Williams was implying everyone can enjoy same-sex relations and fall in love with same-sex partners. A lovely thought when cruising straight trade, but just remember—it works both ways. Love is unpredictable, capricious, and fucking powerful.

Let's address those heterosexual fags and dykes for a second. I'm not talking about bisexuals. I'm not talking about some hulking mouth-breather at Hooters "co-opting queer semiotics" by wearing an earring and saying, "Go girl," or some foxy business babe with a flattop. I'm talking about those people we've all met and joked about but don't quite know what to do with: they're predominantly heterosexual, maybe a little variance here and there but nothing major. But they're campy, promiscuous, play good softball, drive a truck, or do whatever queerish behavior you identify with. Or it may not even be that specific: there's just something you can't put your finger on that sends your gaydar screaming. You muse that maybe they just haven't come out yet, or just haven't met the right person to make them realize their queer potential. They just seem so queer, just like you and me! Substitute straight for queer in that argument and it suddenly sounds all too familiar.

One of my best friends was at times dismissed as a fag hag because she identifies with so much of gay male culture. She's actually far more a fag than a fag hag. We've all heard the line about "a gay man trapped in a woman's body," but I don't mean it here in the usual pejorative sense: sexless and pathetic women, hanging out with gay men they can never have because they're too afraid/ugly to relate to straight men. What a bunch of sexist, internally-homophobic crap. Only psychotic women hang out with fags? Fags are only good enough for second-rate women-friends? Puh-leeze, they are fags, just like the rest of us.

My friend is a stud and a slut. She has no trouble getting men and has had some escapades that put my sexual revolutionary status to shame. She's also never had an unrequited crush on a gay man; it's been the reverse far more frequently. She loves both Pee Wee Herman and Disco Tex and the Sex-o-lettes, and leaped at the chance to go see the Pet Shop Boys in concert with me when all my alterna-fag friends sniffed at the idea. Recently she's gone off and complicated things even more by finding herself this lesbian lover who's a man, but with really sexy femme dyke-type tendencies toward stockings and slips.

Elsewhere on the horizon, the transgender activists are making things even more confusing. How can a rigid Gay Male identity cope with that really cute guy, who used to be a baby butch dyke, and is still involved in a primary relationship with a woman, but considers herself basically a gay man? How do you relate to that foxy dominatrix who's a power femme dyke, but used to be a man? Fuck "relating"—the important issue for a neat 'n' tidy boyfag is: *Which one are you supposed to have sex with?* As it's finally sinking in that if gender is fluid, how can sexual "orientation" not be as well? How can you be rigidly "oriented" toward something that is amorphous, shifting, fluid, tricky, elusive? Basing your identity on sexuality is like building a house on a foundation of pudding.

That's one reason why I think it'd be healthy for many of my fellow fagboys to stop shuddering and wincing at the idea of sex with women, to get over being so neurotically invested in their constructed identity as a Gay Man that the faintest brush of bush threatens them to lengths of misogynist and reactionary overcompensation. I'm not proposing some utopian, idealized state of bisexuality here, I'm just suggesting that a little dose of muff might provoke a healthy reassessment of a sex-based identity. But don't give me the "queer sex is better than straight sex" trope some fags use to consider sex with women without threatening their precious queer identity. That's the line where they'll only consider it if they're being fucked by a butch dyke with a strap-on. Could someone please explain to me how this is different from being fucked by a really butch *straight* woman with a strap-on? Think about this, boys: if it's a dyke, she might invite her girlfriend to join in, but a straight woman might get her boyfriend into the act.

I'm not the first person to say this, but really, if gay men are such sexual outlaws and pioneers of the erotic imagination, what's so goddamn freaky about a little pussy? We love to crow about how any straight man can be had, and cheer them on when they are. Why are we so threatened by the reverse? What are we afraid of losing but an easy answer, a convenient but outmoded identity?

Fucking is not an answer. More realistically, it's a gateway or lens into even more questions, more exploration, and more insight into oneself and society. That's why I'm far more excited these days by ideas running through the bi, transgender, and S/M and kink movements. Instead of protecting territory, engaging in pissing matches and rigidly policing identity boundaries and definitions, they're doing the opposite. They're asking more questions rather than stamping their feet, claiming that they already have the answers. They're pushing issues further, introducing shades of gray. They're forcing us to question whether identity is something that really boils down to a name, label, tag, or definition. Perhaps it's a range of experience. Perhaps it's not one thing at all but several, simultaneous and contradictory, even.

In exploring the complex, fluid, and contradictory identities found within UK gay skinhead subcultures, Murray Healy points out that rigid identities are part and parcel of a conservative, far-right ideology. "The semiotic fundamentalism of skinhead=fascist only serves to reinforce the far right's project of social homogenization and the fixing of identity boundaries.... Fascist ideology is contested by...fluid sexualities" (*Gay Skins: Class, Masculinity, and Queer Appropriation,* Cassell, 1996, p. 145). Fixed, strictly-policed identities are a right-wing project, as are the literal use and zealous protection of symbols and signifiers of those identities. This has been evidenced in the United States, for example, by the far right's fervor against flag burning.

A strain of fascism and conservatism runs through sex-based identities—revealed by the shrillness with which their names and symbols are debated and the vehemence with which their boundaries are policed. However, due to the traditional location of gay rights within leftist politics, the fascist streak inherent in demanding such fixed identities is obscured. But in gay ghettos such as my current home, the normalizing project of building a lesbigay suburban utopia parallel to the sexist, patriarchal original seems apparent. Note what we continue to fight over: perversity; NAMBLA and drag queens in parades; leatherwomen and transgendereds at womyn's music fests. Polymorphous desire and the fluid, non-fixed identities they entail do not allow for the power hierarchies many wish to erect and maintain. Ultimately, identities based on unrealistically stable concepts of sex and gender play into this project too much for my taste. I don't want to be identified, named, pinned down, understood. Those are all the first steps toward manipulation and control.

There are advantages to this fluid alternative, to what must seem like a morass of instability. If we aren't just helpless slaves to our identity, it opens up the philosophical playroom for much more exciting possibilities, such as *choice* and *freedom*. These ideas, in turn, necessitate exploration and articulation of *values* and *responsibilities*. And guess where that leads us? To a field of debate in which we can actually engage the conservative right using their own terms, instead of shrugging our shoulders with a hapless, "We can't help it, this is who we are!"

Homosexuality's over. It was mainly a twentieth-century thang anyway, so let's leave it there. Time's up, kaput. Page me when we get our shit together and have a Sex Celebration Parade or a Take Back the Body March, when we stop dividing and start joining together with others who recognize Western culture is royally fucked when it comes to body, sex, spirit, sensuality, pleasure, and gender. "Queers" are not a distinct minority group neatly parallel to ethnic, religious, or biologically based groups. The issue isn't identity, it's ideology. It's about freedom, responsibility, and values.

DON'T FENCE ME IN:
BI-/PAN-/OMNI-SEXUALS

Before the current Queer Nation there was "the lesbian and gay community," a world in which the bisexual was always problematic—if only because s/he was invisible. The LGBT&F community, and even some queers, aren't necessarily any more comfortable with or accepting of bisexual people, but at least the lingo now writes bisexuals in—bisexuals now have a place in the community that used to forget to acknowledge them.

In reality, the queer community is not as tolerant as it sometimes wants to be. Censured by heterosexual society for being queer, bisexuals are often equally ostracized by homosocial communities for betraying overt or unwritten separatist credos. The queer community seems more accepting of those bisexuals who do not call themselves bisexual: bisexuality has been labeled a subterfuge or a way-station between hetero- and homosexuality for so long that many people instinctively shy away from the term—including many bisexuals themselves.

And since questions of identity do hinge, at least in part, on what we call ourselves, and since the bisexual's identity may in fact be more fluid than the monosexual's, bisexuals make up the largest group of pomosexuals, the queers who are not well-served by essentialist notions of either/or.

In the next two essays, Marco Vassi, the great voyager on the fluid sexual sea, riffs on sexual possibility and its effects on consciousness. Carol Queen shows how bisexuality makes a space for itself in an inhospitable climate, going underground to survive separatism.

BEYOND BISEXUALITY

MARCO VASSI

I.

Sex is a key to doorways of knowing. For me it has been a yoga through which new qualities of self evolved. Like the alchemist who works with a potion for decades and in the process brings about a transmutation of his essence, I spent all my conscious life since the age of eight mixing elements in the crucible of sex, sifting enormous amounts of material to produce a few grams of pure substance. I had fucked or been fucked by over five hundred different women, and twice that many men, in circumstances ranging from brief gaspings in alleys and whorehouses to lengthy relationships. I had gone through all the possible scenarios. And with the suddenness of total change, I became a different kind of person.

At the far edge of bisexuality, I realized that all that had gone before was but the task of perfecting the instrument, the mindbody that is myself. My adventures had served a single purpose: to exhaust all the subjective aspects of the sexual act. The many modes, which had been challenges, areas of exploration, were now my tools—homosexuality, heterosexuality, bisexuality, abstruse psychosexual states and practices, the so-called perversions, the many masks of libidinal displacement...these were now at my command, to be used the way a director uses a cast of characters to realize a vision.

Having no term which encompassed the totality of my erotic awareness and function, I found it necessary to coin a new word, and thus formulated the concept: metasexuality.

II.

Metasexual consciousness is born once one has healed the internal male-female duality. Strictly speaking, only those who have attained that state are capable of understanding it. But in the same way that the Buddha nature inheres in every living thing, and enlightenment is simply a waking up to what we have been all along, metasexuality is manifested in all human beings whether they know it or not. But to see this involves at least an intellectual effort, that of making the distinction between metasex and sex itself.

Sex is that activity which takes place between one man and one woman who are fucking to make a baby. Metasex is everything else. This is gone into full detail in *"The Metasexual Manifesto"* [in *Metasex, Mirth and Madness* by Marco Vassi], so I won't elaborate here. In this essay, I would like only to suggest some of what is uncovered once that crucial distinction is made. For once we cease applying the laws of sex to metasex, metasex reveals itself as a rich and unexplored territory.

The most blatant example of confusion between the two vehicles lies at the core of every historical civilization and consists of the prejudice that two is the *natural* number for the erotic encounter. Metasexual awakening challenges this principle head on. This notion is obviously valid for the sexual realm but proves completely erroneous in the metasexual worldview. The assumption that *two* allows the most perfect erotic union is a misconception rooted in primitive bisexual consciousness.

When one transcends male-female dualism, eroticism becomes susceptible of a more subtle mathematical understanding. For each number, there is a different and unique quality of consciousness, and no one is intrinsically superior to any of the others.

One, the single point, metasex of no dimension. This is the realm of masturbation, that poorly understood activity, usually considered an aberration, but actually a powerful vehicle in its own right. To masturbate to full orgasm (not merely ejaculation or clitoral twitching, but full vegetative release) is a sublime and solitary act, requiring capacity for fear and awe. To bring about one's own orgasm, without the company of others, without fantasies to mask the facticity of the deed, requires great inner resources.

One has certain shadings, for a person can masturbate in the presence of others and vary the nature of the experience. Masturbating while another assists by giving positive reinforcement, kissing, stroking, speaking, is a profound means of grasping the reality of self and other. How many couples, thinking themselves uninhibited, are unable to masturbate in one another's presence? It is not going too far to suggest that unless an individual has come to terms with one, he or she will lack full capability in the higher numbers.

Two is the official sexual model of our civilization, entrenched in our archetypal mind. It is, however, from a metasexual viewpoint, nothing more than the metasex of a single line, the metasex of one dimension: it is totally flexible since a line can assume an infinity of curves yet always remain in one dimension.

A————————————**B**

With *two* accepted as the ideal, the "natural" way of doing things, the other numbers get relegated to the categories of sin, crime, perversion, or diversion. Even many sophisticates measure their orgies against an unconscious norm. Again, this is because they have not yet dealt with the internal bisexual split.

The enforced exclusivity of the number even damages the couple-form itself. As people try to squeeze all erotic exploration into that single format, it suffers from a fatal overload. It is as though, with the integral calculus available to us, a law was passed forbidding us to do anything but count on our fingers and toes.

Two has its uses, its value, and its delights, as well as its limitations. Biologically, it is the vehicle of procreation. And it possesses a certain classic purity of line which makes it attractive to radicals as well as traditionalists. Perhaps its major appeal lies in its comparative simplicity.

Three is the first number in the metasex of two dimensions, metasex of the plane. *Three* must be understood as more than the addition of one more to the basic two. It involves a whole new quality of consciousness, something which cannot come about with people who are still thinking in male-female terms.

The fact of the new dimension becomes clear when one sees that within a triangle, the twosome is but one element of the greater vehicle. In a triangle, in fact, there are seven elementary constituent parts:

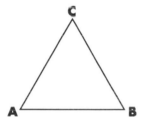

Individuals: A, B, C; couples: AB, AC, BC; and the overall form: ABC.

In theory, the triangle is equilateral; in practice, there are many functional variations. Differences in body type, age, astronomic factors, genetic determinations, and so forth, each produce a new triangle. It is the constant tension between the complexity of human dynamics and the inherent properties of a given number which gives the metasexual act its defining nature. The amount of energy available gives it its scope. This can be stated as a general principle: any metasexual act is a function of energy, personality, and geometry.

Four is a difficult number. From one angle, it is two squared. Thus, many couples attempting different numbers before having come to terms with the bisexual split go to *four*, where they do nothing more than intensify their basic dualistic basis.

In another sense, four is the next two-dimensional figure after three, having one more side than a triangle. As such, it offers fifteen elementary units. As follows:

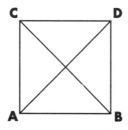

Individuals: A, B, C, D; couples: AB, AC, AD, BC, BD, CD; triangles: ABC, ABD, ACD, BCD; and the overall form: ABCD. The richness of this structure is grasped when one realizes that not only are all of these sub-units operating simultaneously, but all personality components are functioning, and at the high energy level four people can generate. This gives a strong, continually changing, multileveled reality which only a very few are capable of experiencing and integrating.

But further, *four* is the first number which yields three dimensions:

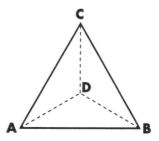

A pyramid with a triangular base. To answer the question as to what makes the difference in any group between a plane with four sides and a pyramid is outside the scope of this article. But one can see that the reality of the metasexual fourth dimension, a spacetime of Einsteinian eroticism, would be the next step in this direction.

I am not personally qualified to discuss the numbers from *five* upward since I have not experienced them, except in gatherings of swingers who had not yet realized their metasexual nature and were piling bodies on without changing the essential consciousness of the act.

It is also fascinating to wonder whether *zero,* or metacelibacy, may be seen not as a renunciation but as an embrace of all metasex.

III.

There was a time when it seemed to people that the sun revolved around the earth, a view enshrined in the Ptolemaic model of the solar system. Now, with a less parochial view, we have developed a new understanding, signaled by the introduction of the Copernican model.

The introduction of the metasexual paradigm is no less a shift in the history of our evolving understanding. The vast majority of the species has not seen past the conditioned strictures of the number *two.* And even those in the vanguard, having their orgies, still operate from the standpoint of a male-female dualism. The most sophisticated among them proclaim themselves bisexuals, not aware that this is the dead-end of that particular tunnel vision. The only way out is to go within to heal the internal split. A monad has no gender.

The question now presents itself: what form does the metasexual lifestyle take?

I won't presume an answer. As for myself, I currently allow circumstances to guide me. Having no prejudices, no preconceptions, I am open to whatever is possible, to whoever wants to dance with me. Yet, if this is a genuine satori, as I practice the living awareness of it, a specific form may evolve. It is possible that I might one day accept a simple pattern to express my true nature: perhaps an uncomplicated heterosexual linear bond, or perhaps a gay threesome, or a life of introspective masturbation. For, if one has subsumed all forms, then one is free to manifest in any form whatsoever.

Beyond bisexuality, externals take on a different meaning than when one is caught in the male-female duality. Even the most stereotyped act is permeated with a brilliant awareness that transforms the perception of reality.

BEYOND THE VALLEY
OF THE FAG HAGS

CAROL QUEEN

Falling in love with fags is falling for make-believe. That's why a lot of women do it. Even my own dear clueless mother once had a romance with a sweet young man who used to play duets with her in piano stores during the dark days of World War II. "He never laid a hand on me," she recalled, and I had my suspicions as she told me this story—confirmed when she added that he always used to like double-dating, and sometimes the boys would leave the girls alone at the table to go off to the restroom together....

"Mom, he was gay!" I yelled, proud to have sniffed out yet another of my kind across the boundaries of time and space.

"Do you really think so?" wondered Mom.

My own mom, a proto-fag hag.

If pressed, many fag hags would probably express relief that the objects of their affection never lay a hand on them. Handsome fags offer all the girl talk and none of the testosterone poisoning, making great boyfriends for women who'd rather keep physical intimacy at bay. But from my very first love-struck relationship with a gay man, I wanted more. I wanted it all.

Sorry about the language I'm using here. I'm well aware that both "fag" and "fag hag" are pejoratives, the latter perhaps even more unequivocally than the former. But I came out with men who were reclaiming antigay hate speech with classically campy flair and with a leftist bent born of Stonewall, which had happened only five years before. They said "fag," so I said "fag"; I said "dyke," and we all said "queer," a couple of decades before Queer Nation.

No one was trying to reclaim or redeem fag hags. I came out before I was eighteen, and already I was trying to figure out if that phrase was supposed to describe me. But I was also a dyke, though not a very accomplished one—I couldn't find a girlfriend to save my life, and so I hung out with the boys, much preferring their brand of sisterhood to that dished out down at the Womyn's Coffee House. When I finally did find a lover she turned out to be a bigger fag hag than me, and it wouldn't be too melodramatic to say that she was using me to get next to gay men. That wouldn't have been so bad, but she stopped having sex with me almost as soon as she started.

Actually, my first queer sex had been not with a woman, but with a fag. He was my high school lit teacher, and I'd been laying for him since well before graduation. This was intensely consternating to him, because I don't think a woman had ever expressed interest in him before. He really was the sort of man that only a woman who was a fag hag could love: a fey little chipmunk who wore antique suits and, I think, despaired that he was born into this era instead of in a time when he might have had a shot at hobnobbing (or more) with Oscar Wilde. I adored him completely. Fags are a different species of man, and he was my first fag. He taught me how to dish and loaned me his precious copy of that precious classic, *Song of the Loon.*

And eventually we wound up in bed—though not before sharing a boy or two: he would flirt with them, and I would have sex with them and tell him how it went. But one night he got the two of us poisonously drunk on MD 2020 *(that's* how nervous he was), rented us a motel room, and we tried to fuck. I remember only that his underwear was as iconoclastically antique as the rest of his clothes and that he murmured (shortly before we both passed out), "The musculature of your back is really lovely."

Those were his exact words, and I treasured them then as I do now, as a gender-bent talisman of a queer kind of attraction. If only either of us had known there are more models than heterosexual for a male and a female who want to exchange erotic energy. For us, the expectation that sex would equal fucking meant we had to drunkenly jettison the whole attempt, though I am convinced that he loved me as much as I loved him. We just couldn't figure out what that was supposed to mean, much less what we were supposed to *do*.

Fags are a different species of man. I came further and further out as a dyke, eventually finding a girlfriend who loved and desired me (and bemusedly tolerated my unnaturally high fag quotient in a small dyke community where women weren't encouraged to be friends with men at all). Even as I systematically wrote men out of my life, gay men were always exceptions. During my Birkenstock years I was sure I would never have a deep relationship with a man again—but a feminist utopia without fags? If I couldn't surround myself with fags, girlfriend, I didn't want any part of your revolution.

I see now, of course, that I kept my bisexuality alive during that decade via subsumed erotic relationships with gay men. If in my politics I conveniently forgot that fags were men at all, my libido remembered, and I simmered with lust and love for one after the other as the '70s waned and the '80s dawned.

I felt safe with them from the slings and arrows of sex-role stereotypes. I listened raptly to tales of secret cocksucking forays in the park and bathhouse expeditions to Portland or San Francisco. I continued at every opportunity to sneak looks at their porn. I learned how to dance, dish, and dress like a girl. I suffered (and never got over it) when my new girlfriend didn't love Will, then my best gay male friend, as much as I did. (I'm not certain he was thrilled with her either.) I am ashamed to say that that jealousy breached my relationship with him, since, as a dyke, the one thing that was out of bounds was to choose loyalty to fags over loyalty to my lovers.

I got (and continue to get) two priceless gifts from gay men—support for my own queerness and a vision of maleness very different from the testosterone-poisoned version I grew up with. In this latter realm the "fag-as-(platonic)-girlfriend" phenomenon held great importance. In a small dyke community, you couldn't dish your girlfriend problems with another woman—it would probably turn into a star-crossed, dyke-dramalicious love affair. Het boys tended to leer without understanding the emotional import of the situation. Straight girls understood the emotion, but then they'd want to have an affair too. No, a girl needed fags around.

What was the difference between me and a fag hag? Surely most important was my queerness. I was in the club. That made for connections stronger and more playful than anything I'd felt before. I think fag hags are attracted, often, by gay men's unattainability; like my mom, they find fags safe. They would, if really erotically focused on fags, like somehow to craft a recognizable heterosexual relationship with one, while I want a queer connection, a reminder that boys and girls don't have to play those tired old games even when they choose to play with each other. I would gladly be a fag too, in fact; my very femaleness is (at least on the surface) open to negotiation.

If only I didn't look so underage when I cross-dress. (I know, that's a plus in some circles. But that's another essay.)

Shared queer identity notwithstanding, it took me years to understand that my attraction to gay men did not need to imply a hetero attraction or outcome. If anything, I subsumed my erotic feelings for fags because I understood fagness as a rejection of all things het—if not female. My boundaries were up because I was confused by the implications of reciprocal attraction. I certainly didn't want to make any fag straight, even a little bit. Yet I had no models for queer male/female relating, and for some reason I did not run into bisexual men, who might have helped me challenge my assumptions about the boy/girl, gay/straight problem. Looking back, it seems surprising (and not very clear-sighted) that I wasn't learning from my experiences as a dyke: living in that world taught me deep lessons about female possibility, a potent antidote to the circumscribed notions about femaleness my culture had tried to give me. Well, to be fair, I was learning, but the lessons were taught in a gynocentric classroom. None of the other women I knew seemed to need, as I did, to wrestle with the question of where fags fit into their lives.

Too, those were not days in which gender was seen as a permeable membrane. Dyke feminism wasn't ready to grapple with those issues yet, and so the dialogue about gender identity—which opened for me new ways of looking at my life with fags—had not yet begun. In those days, girls would not be boys, nor was sympathy expressed for boys who would be girls, especially among the Michigan Womyn's Music Festival-going set whose philosophy carried the day.

So I managed for a while to tell myself, against no small amount of evidence, that my relationships with fags were less important than the ones I was having with women. I was out of college, no longer active in the mixed gay/lesbian groups that had served to throw me into intense proximity with gay men, whose wit, incisive minds, and passionate politics thrilled me. There were fewer gay men in my life then than there had been since I was fifteen years old.

And in those years AIDS was brewing.

I grew aware of AIDS gradually. Then I began wondering and worrying about all my friends and beloved ones from years gone by: Alan, Brett, Jai, Will, Jimmy, Buzzi, Dee, Chrys, Frank, Roan Pony, Charles, and so many more: the boys from Gay Youth, the men from Gay People's Alliance and Stonewall Day Alliance, Eugene Citizens for Human Rights, and Faggots Against Fascism.

I had volunteered for every queer organization my town had ever seen, and I now joined the organizing body of the Willamette AIDS Council. I spent Sunday afternoons learning the strange new art of coalition building with nice ladies from the plasma center and straight doctors from the health department, taking weekend-long workshops to learn the weird unsettling science of T-cells and Western Blot blood tests. There I met James, a sweet, funny, owlish fag with a mind like a steel trap—the attorney whose politicking impelled Oregon to divest its state pension fund money from investments in South Africa. Gently, in the interstices between our committee work and bylaws-crafting, James let me fall in love with him.

I used my love for James to power my AIDS work: whenever I felt overwhelmed or afraid I thought of him and launched into another speech, sat through another meeting. I used it, too, to finally challenge the boundaries between man and woman, gay and straight, I'd let my community erect around me. What was safely subsumed was now in danger of disappearing, and our relationship was erotic in the flesh as none of my relationships with gay men had ever been, though we retained total clarity that he was a fag and I a dyke. Through James, I let myself feel the true intensity of my feelings for fags.

This was far from easy, for two main reasons. I lived in a world in which men, by definition, had cooties. Against the evidence of his response to me, I believed that in James' world women had cooties too, which didn't exactly fill me with confidence. One night we danced together in the town's one gay bar. I took hold of his necktie, pulled him to me, and there in front of all the other queers, electrically, confusingly, we kissed. Who were we then? Stared at by everyone, who could we be? We made jokes about what bad queers we were, but joking covered over deep fear: we both loved (and needed) our community, its structure, its support. We were misbehaving. What would become of us?

Even more primally, the thought of being sexual opened onto the unknown. How were we to connect? Who would begin? What would we do? Our gender and sexual identities did not lead us toward each other, but away. To make matters more complicated still, we were (I realize now) both bottoms.

Ironically, in the charged circle of AIDS activism, a place from within which we advocated open sexual communication, our fear and confusion silenced us. I assumed he wanted cock, and grieved (for the only time in my life) that I didn't have one. He might have been more afraid that I was seronegative than turned off by my female parts. But I'll never know: I never asked, never uttered words that, had they been spoken, might have breached the wall of silence erected between our gender- and orientation-coded bodies. And so our love affair was both passionate and chaste; we kissed so long we steamed up the windows of the car, slept together with our underwear on, and when he died I was left weighted down with what I had wanted to give him.

He was not the only one of my beloved fags who died, nor even the first. Roan Pony, Dee, John, David, Tede, Brian, James, Ted—one by one, lights went out. AIDS has not been kind to fag hags. In our virginal romances, the script did not call for widowhood. We were all supposed to fade gracefully together, taking turns bringing champagne for the mimosas.

If only either James or I had understood that there are more models than the heterosexual one for a male and female who want to exchange erotic energy. My relationship with James was deep and real, putting the lie forever to my glib protestations that I could never love a man. I began to see that even if I never fucked one, my love for fags put me in territory technically outside the bounds of the Lesbian Nation. It was time to resurrect what had been subsumed: my bisexual identity and my openness to men. I did not want to lose another man I did not have the courage to love all the way.

A lot of straight men love bisexual women, for a lot of reasons—including admirable impulses away from ultra-hetero roles. (Most feminists have missed a salient organizing tool by not realizing how many men also rankle under the weight of sex-role stereotypes; the National Organization for Women just doesn't know what to do with men who would really rather be lesbians.) It's taken me several years to understand a little bit about the men who—there's not even a name for them, as there is for fag hags—desire and identify with queer women. But even these straight men had one big handicap in my book—they were straight. A man only really started to interest me after he'd had a dick in his mouth. When it came to pursuing intimacy with men, I already had a model: I loved fags.

I literally had met only one bisexual but gay-identified man before I moved to San Francisco. It was in the '70s, the decade when even gays gave lip service to the naturalness of the bisexual option, and Chrys and I had a stormy little affair as we both got more queer—a trajectory that, while mutual, ultimately moved us further apart. But in San Francisco I started to meet bisexual men who were plenty queer just as they were: bisexual activist and leatherman David Lourea, whose domestic partner was a gay man; Leland, in whose company I finally achieved my desire to be a trashy bathhouse fag (as well as to consider whether I wanted to be a parent, a question I thought my queer life had directed me away from forever); and finally, Robert.

Robert—possessor of the most inspiringly arcane sex history I had ever heard—became my fag-come-true. He introduced himself to me as someone's "twinkie"—a word straight men know only in conjunction with junk-food binges (and the occasional resulting homicidal attack committed by the likes of Dan White). He haunted bathhouses before his high school graduation. He taught me that a quick cure for penis envy (in any size, shape, and color) could be purchased at Good Vibrations and that women do not have the market cornered on fuckable orifices. A leather daddy crossed with a lingerie-wearing butt slut, he preferred his sex and gender cues all shook up. Deeply queer, he hates the p.c.-speak that would call our community "Lesbian/Gay/Bi/Trans and Friends"— because he's a little bit of all of it and has no desire to see his sexuality fractionalized.

Clearly, the man of my dreams.

Have I just landed the biggest pervert in town, a polymorphous boundary-free zone—or does he represent (and inspire me to be) a new kind of "don't-fence-me-in" queer who grew up to challenge the notion of "opposite" sexes, Tarzan-and-Jane gender roles, and cootified cunts and cocks? I hope it's the latter, for I know both of us had been lonely living the left-of-hetero life without a real community to embrace us, and I know many other queers (and bent heterosexuals) who were and are similarly isolated.

I wish I had known about this space between gay and straight in time to seal my love for James with more than a kiss. And I hope we queers can be pioneers again in this, as we have in so many other arenas; I hope we can help heal the breach between men and women by allowing love *and* desire to flourish whenever and however it takes root; that we can see through and deconstruct our bi- and "heterophobia" as we (rightfully) demand that hets dismantle their homophobia; that we can go coed with Whitman's "blessed love of comrades." Falling in love with fags (*and* falling in love with women) has meant to me, at bottom, falling in love with queer comrades, falling in love with the chance to question the culture's rigid authoritarianism and its unhealthy dichotomies, of which "gay/straight" is really no more progressive an example than "male/female."

I hope, too, that we can truly come to be an army of lovers, for an army of lovers cannot fail. I do not want this community to be simply an alliance; alliances can be broken. I want it to be a deep, dizzying, expectation-defying love affair.

THROUGH A GLASS QUEERLY:
OUR BOYS, OURSELVES

In compiling this anthology (as in living our lives) we were inspired by the lives and writings of queers who, even during a fairly rigid era as far as identity politics were concerned, refused to be cookie cutter copies of everyone else in the tribe. Two of the most influential of these authors, Pat Califia and Dorothy Allison, write about a topic that has been taboo throughout most modern lesbian history: loving and appreciating queer men.

There are certainly queer men who appreciate and have been influenced by queer women—and as soon as this anthology is published, no doubt, we're going to hear from plenty of them—but the fact remains that in contemporary "gay and lesbian" and "LGBT&F" culture, radical lesbian feminism has made intimacy with men, including queer men, more taboo than love for women has been for most men; queer men have also shaped a more outrageous, public sexual culture than most women have had access to. For both these reasons the subject of gay male sexuality has been a fitting inquiry for women with a transgressive bent.

Too, the most rigid years of identity politics—coinciding, ironically enough, with right-wing ascendancy in government—began to break down for dykes partly because of the depredations into our queer community of the AIDS epidemic. Women assumed caretaking and activist roles rooted in their regard for gay men. If gay men had a parallel breakthrough of understanding about the role of women in their lives (and many of them doubtless did), it was vastly overshadowed by the toll the epidemic has taken. Yet for many lesbians and gay men, HIV put the first nail in the coffin of separatism.

IDENTITY SEDITION AND PORNOGRAPHY

PAT CALIFIA

I've adopted many personas as an author of sexually-explicit fiction: gay and straight, male and female, top and bottom, and categories in between those binaries. For more than ten years, I wrote an advice column for *The Advocate*'s classified section, which many readers assumed was penned by a gay man, and I also wrote "The Sexpert" advice column for *Advocate Men*. In 1992, I spent a pleasant year working at Liberation Publications Inc. as the editor of all their erotic titles. By editing the pansexual anthology *Doing It for Daddy*, I have encouraged gay, bisexual, and straight people to look for fantasy material outside of the boundaries of their own sexual orientation. And, of course, I've frequently been accused of contaminating lesbian culture and sexuality with evil things like casual sex, porn, or S/M that were supposed to be relegated to the breeders and fags.

I've received more than one fan letter from lesbian readers who complain about my propensity to write about male characters and women who are not dykes. One woman said, "It's not that I can fault the quality of this work; it's just that there's so little material for lesbians. The need is so great." Lesbian invisibility is a really horrible thing. It is awful to look around and wonder, where am I, where did I come from, where are my people, how come we have been kept from each other this way?

But I believe that when I color outside the lines and draw non-lesbian attention to my work, I am also fighting our invisibility. Writing about people who I was not was a way for me to escape the dreadful pink ghetto of lesbian fiction. It's appalling that most so-called lesbian fiction appears to be written for an eighth-grade reading level. The bulk of lesbian literature is a form of juvenile literature. Not only that, it's apparently written and published by people who don't particularly like kids or think they're very smart.

I've been accused of trying to deceive gay men by masquerading as one, and I've gotten more than one unhappy letter from a gay male reader who feels violated by a female presence in his jackoff fantasies. One of them wrote, "What I want to know is, how can you know so much about what I want to see when I look at another man? How do you know what makes me feel that I must submit to him? And how do you know what it feels like to get my cock sucked or fuck another man? You can't know these things. It just isn't possible." I don't know, maybe it's leakage from past lives. I seem to have all these memories of being various sorts of men, usually not very nice ones.

Of course, there are also lesbians who are convinced that "Pat Califia" is really the pseudonym of an evil straight man or fag (or, even more heinous, a bisexual bitch) who is trying to besmirch and twist the lesbian community to his or her own perverted ends, and gay men who can't see anything erotic about the genderfucking material that I've set in their own community. Rumors have also circulated that I am transgendered, in either or both directions.

Just to set the record straight: I am a female-bodied person who writes about every kind of person I can imagine. Although I briefly contemplated sex reassignment when I was much younger, I decided that would not resolve my gender conflicts. I'm never sure if I have gender dysphoria or species dysphoria. I often try to explain that I'm really a starfish trapped in a human body and I'm very new to your planet. Or that in fact I am a woman trapped in a man's body, which really confuses other people but makes sense to me.

Part of what gender dysphoria is about is coming up against the really crazy walls between male and female experience in our culture. There's so much mythology about inherent and intrinsic differences that is not accurate. It makes sense for us as activists and writers to confront that wherever we find it and try to figure out if there are differences and how important—or inconsequential—they are. One of the things fiction can do for us is take us for brief journeys, even if they're just imaginary journeys, inside each other's bodies. If you have not traveled inside another person's physical reality, you do not know what their life is about.

Most of the time, I write about dykes, because that is the community I politically and sexually affiliate with; but I have fantasies about men, women, and others; and wherever my libido goes, the keyboard is sure to follow. Butch dykes with male fantasy personas populate stories like "The Calyx of Isis" and "Daddy." *Macho Sluts,* my first collection of short stories, includes "The Spoiler," a story about a leatherman who specializes in topping tops, and "The Surprise Party," a faux-rape scene in which three leathermen in cop uniforms provide a leatherdyke with quite an elaborate birthday present. My second collection of short stories, *Melting Point,* includes "Unsafe Sex," a morality tale about a white guppie (a gay male yuppie) who goes slumming for sleazy anonymous public sex with a black leatherman, and "Fix Me Up," an SF story in which a straight male submissive puts his life in danger by getting too close to a sadistic dyke sex worker and junkie whose community has been decimated by a disease that resembles AIDS. There's also "Belonging," the tale of a homophobic straight man's abduction and re-education at the hands of a leather master, published in *Advocate Men* and anthologized in John Preston's *Flesh and the Word* and Susie Bright's *Best American Erotica 1993.* And I have two stories about a gay male vampire, "The Wolf is My Shepherd, I Shall Not Want," in Carol Queen and Lawrence Schimel's *Switch Hitters,* and "Parting Is Such Sweet Sorrow," in Michael Rowe and Thomas S. Roche's anthology *Sons of Darkness.*

Some of the gay male fiction I write is intended for a gay male audience. But I believe there are more lesbians who read my gay male pornography than gay men. Most of the time, then, I write gay men's pornography for women. And I think that makes it a little different than standard gay male stroke-lit. I'm always really happy when gay men find the stuff I write effective or say that it rings true for them. But I also have a little humility about that. I know that there are parts of male experience that I can't access. Empathy can only take you so far.

Mainstream culture certainly doesn't encourage us to write about queer desire at all, let alone jump the fence and try to capture the experience of other sexual or gender minorities. Gay male and lesbian culture is obsessed with purity of identity as the only basis for figuring out who you can trust or dance with. This creates a lavender breed of segregationism. So why bother? Why be a dyke author who writes man-to-man smut? I could have written gay male and heterosexual pornography under pseudonyms and cashed my checks without rocking anybody's preconceptions about gender and sexual orientation. Exactly.

I am not just a writer. I am an activist. Writing porn under a pseudonym felt depressing to me. I know a lot of writers still do this to finance their "serious" work. While I can understand the need to protect oneself from being trivialized or ostracized by the literary establishment, this still seems like cheating to me. If your name is not on your work, you never get held accountable for it. So you are bound to get lazy and do some bad writing. I've used pseudonyms for my published fiction only when a given magazine's policies required it. There wasn't much of a kick for me in writing straight porn from the point of view of a heterosexual man or woman, unless it was clear that a dyke was creating this material. Straight people blithely assume it's their prerogative to write about us; but we know a lot more about them than they know about us. We came out of them. Most of us made a rather extensive study of heterosexuality before leaving it behind. Even after we come out, we have to be experts in straight presumption, ignorance, and frailty in order to survive.

By writing about heterosexual desire, I appropriate portions of that experience, which are supposed to be universal, normal, and right, and create an ironic commentary upon it. How "natural" can heterosexuality be if a lesbian, merely by studying its artifacts, can create a facsimile of straight smut? I sometimes say that I like to watch straight pornography because it is the most exotic thing I can imagine, men and women being sexual with one another, and I don't quite understand how that could really work. But this isn't completely accurate. I'm just looking for ways to convey my conviction that, whatever my motivation is for being turned on to straight porn, it certainly isn't because heterosexuality has been ordained by ghod and biology to dominate my imagination. Instead, I like to think I have objectified or fetishized these images, and by evaluating them from a lesbian perspective, taken away their power to intimidate or outrank me.

All-boy porn presents a different challenge to me as a lesbian author. First of all, there is a component of gay male culture which is invested in maintaining male privilege. Thus, we see the sort of gay man who becomes politically active because he is outraged to discover that, simply because he has sex with other men, there are people and institutions attempting to deny him the dick-based privilege he believes is his due. Someone who was politicized by this process does not easily make alliances with other oppressed groups. This view of gay male sexuality constitutes a sort of boy's club, a world from which women must be rigorously excluded because of their inferiority and unattractiveness. Out of this comes gay male porn that has weird misogynist asides, as if denigrating women's bodies was a sort of foreplay.

Of course, as a feminist, I find this deeply offensive. While I acknowledge that men and women have some biological and genetic differences, I believe that many of the differences we think are most important are in fact socially constructed. It isn't people's body parts that give them social power or disenfranchise them; it's the significance we all attach to those naughty bits. If the penis is going to be elevated to semidivine status as a marker for the freedom and self-importance that men enjoy, I think it's natural for someone who wants to overturn the patriarchy to get behind one of the damn things and see how it feels to drive it. Separatism has been a more popular strategy than appropriation for lesbian feminists. But I believe that attempts to eliminate or quarantine the penis and its bearers perpetuate a notion that men or the male sex organ are special. Demonization lends as much power as idealization, if not more.

There is an enormous body of texts and images that can educate any willing spectator about what sorts of sensations, visions, and emotions gay men expect to experience as part of their sexuality. I happen to think I have an unusual level of empathy with other people's somatic experiences; but even if I did not, simply perusing the discourse would give me enough ammunition to get my reader to hit his target with a perfect cum shot every time. In conventional pornography, and in most sexual encounters, what people actually experience matters less than what they'd like to experience or what they assume they should feel, do, or say. The discourse of pleasure is often more influential than any individual's lived experience of a particular sensation or partner. Of course, I don't want to stop with the expected or the preprogrammed. I want to use enough of the typical to lull the reader into receptivity, then use his or her arousal to seduce and terrify with new ideas, unfamiliar territory, surprising fantasy icons who didn't get their lines from the latest insipid video of highly tanned, coke-sniffing gymbot cocksuckers.

If I had written only about women doing S/M with other women, I could have claimed a privileged place for that material, as describing activity devoid of male presence and therefore supposedly devoid of oppression. There are still some members of the lesbian S/M community who feel very strongly that S/M between lesbian feminists is okay, but it's violence and misogyny when anybody else does it. If I had been able to come out into a leather dyke community, perhaps I would share this elitist view. But I had to create my own tribe from scratch, and I got much more support for that from gay men, heterosexual sadomasochists, bisexual women, and professional dominants than I did even from other leatherdykes. I am a pretty traditional person in some ways. I believe in respecting your origins, your elders, and my elders were not wise old lesbians who had been doing bondage and whipping for decades before I came along. I've always known how much I have in common with other perverts, how hard we all struggle to come to a place where we can have self-respect, love, and fun in our lives, and there's no reason to erase that knowledge. The larger society would like us to remain divided, fragmented, and suspicious of one another. I believe lesbian sexuality is not a secret we have to keep to protect its specialness. I do not lose my power as a dyke when I put my cunt (or cock) in other people's faces: I get it back, tripled.

These politics are based on personal experiences with crossing all kinds of boundaries and combining categories of people and erotic experiences in what were, in the beginning, new and unusual ways. In a way, becoming a pervert without a community was a privilege, because it forced me to gain access to "private" moments that otherwise would have eluded my witness. The way I felt the first time I saw two men have sex with each other was a defining moment for me, and that remains the core of my motivation for exploring male homosexuality in print. It's hard to go back that far, but it was one of the more important moments of my life.

It happened during a Christmas party at the Catacombs, a fist-fucking club that occupied the basement flat of Steve McEachern's three-story Victorian house. I was dating Cynthia Slater, a bisexual woman who was also a professional dominant and a fag hag. She had hooked up with some of the more drug-enhanced and sexually outrageous leathermen, and if I was going to hang out with her, I had to figure out how to hang out with them as well. My memory of this weekend is somewhat hazy, as huge quantities of alcohol, pot, poppers, MDA, speed, and acid were going around, and at the time I was an equal-opportunity stoner. The first night I was there, the boys (sensing my unfamiliarity with their colorful and excessive sexual style) sent Cynthia and me downstairs to play all by ourselves. I do remember, quite vividly, going downstairs the next day to the elaborate three-room dungeon with one of Steve's ex-lovers, who instructed me in the fine art of getting my fist up his ass and keeping it there for what seemed like hours. And thinking, as I felt the smooth and obviously fragile membranes cling to my wrist and lower arm, that this certainly did not feel like the few awkward and weird attempts I'd made at heterosexual intercourse before coming out as a dyke. After my maiden voyage on the Good Ship Crisco, the boys figured I could deal with anything, so the play space was thrown open to all of Steve's holiday house guests.

Perhaps I was able to view the wild and frantic male coupling that went on with such equanimity because I was so thoroughly medicated. The fact that it resembled dyke sex was another bridge into the polymorphous perverse territory of empathy. Everybody at the Catacombs was usually much too stoned to make use of his dick. Sex involved hands and buttholes and mouths. At a typical party, cocks might regain their ability to get hard after four or five a.m., when most everyone's drugs were wearing off. Then you would see some rough cock-sucking and dick-fucking.

Most of these men were young, muscular, marked with tattoos or piercings. The leather they wore and the metal and ink they put in their bodies were not fashion statements, they were brave declarations of difference and affirmations of a passion for pain, power, and extreme degrees of penetration. Some of these signals and tokens were fated to become clichés, but that was hardly apparent then. When I try to see them in my memory, my mind's eye becomes misty. Substitute images of wild horses or cougars come instead of the faces and bodies of my beloved dead. Sometimes I think all of the really beautiful men have died. That of course is not true; it is simply my heart's reluctance to form new attachments, a desire to withdraw from human contact as a way to avoid the pain of loss in the future.

In part, I continue to write gay male porn because I refuse to give in to grief. I'm always aware of the bodies of the people we've lost that we all walk over every time we find each other in the dark. And that some of what we do when we encounter each other is save them as well as ourselves. My sexuality and my pornography are a living memorial. It has become more important than ever to validate the inherent worth and holiness of the force that draws one man to another, and I may seem like a rather odd choice for the prophet of this gospel, but I think the next generation of queer young men needs to get this affirmation from as many sources as possible.

A lot of negative and nasty stuff has been written about Castro clones and butch posturing, as if castigating fag fashion of the '70s and '80s would recover the lives that have been scythed down by AIDS. Like any fad or trend, it certainly had aspects of being boring, controlling, and regimented. But it was also liberatory. The notion that gay men could be masculine was very important to the early development of gay activism and liberation. Even queens talked about themselves as "getting butch" whenever they fought back. Yes, this is sexist, but I am grateful for any change in self-concept that encouraged us as a persecuted group of people to stop fighting with each other and start kicking ass when we were threatened. Certainly I think gay men at that time, as now, could benefit from a more conscious critique of the pitfalls of masculinity. But for my friends, hanging on to their masculinity was a way to be strong and prideful as well as gay.

S/M and casual sex were components of that healing process. Gay men of that time were determined to own their own bodies and control their own lives. They wanted to live without shame and without limits. They took great liberties and, without permission or assistance, built a vibrant culture that was full of pride, pleasure, art, and radical politics. It's become fashionable to rag on "bathhouse culture" for its putative selfishness, irresponsibility, immaturity, racism, sexism, and inability to deal with aging. That's fair comment, but it's also Monday morning quarterbacking. And in the part of the leather community where I was hanging out, there was an outspoken rejection of racism, a surprising amount of openness to women and their issues, a warm affirmation of the potential attractiveness of at least some older men, and a stated desire to care for one another if we got sick, queerbashed, fired, or arrested.

Without the fraternal model of the leather community and the long tradition of charitable work among drag queens in their court system, the larger gay community would have been even harder hit by the AIDS pandemic. If an accurate history of our response to the plague is ever written, it will have to acknowledge the pivotal role played by leather-men in forming the first organizations to respond to AIDS. Certainly the S/M community in general has done an amazing job of educating its members about safer sex, in part because we already had an ethic about taking care of one another, communicating honestly about our limits and desires, and an open attitude about using equipment to enhance our physical and psychic experiences during sessions.

But I digress. As I said earlier, when I try to go that far back in memory, my mind slides sideways, fearing the intensity of recalling the past. Writers have to learn to recognize that moment when we glaze over. It's always a cue that something important is being buried alive. But everything we've ever seen continues to happen in some timeless place within our consciousness. You can recapture anything.

As I saw these men engaged in an erotic ballet with one another at Steve's holiday party, thinking of nothing else except the look, taste, and feel of one another's bodies, I started to cry. There was nothing revolting there. Nothing wrong, inferior, sick, or strange. Instead, something beautiful and powerful was happening. The act had its own value, integrity, and meaning. I thought this was the sort of energy that potentially had the power to transform the whole world for the better. It had potential to heal and to make the nature of men and women more sane. I still feel that way about it, I still feel that there's something sacred and awesome about men loving each other and having a lust connection with each other. So much of the evil that men do comes from their self-hatred and their fear of one another. Who else cares enough about men to fix the huge problem of male violence and abuse? I believe that gay men have a spiritual vocation to transform themselves and the nature of manhood. And by that, I do not mean become feminine, or become women, or become third-gender. Those are entirely different paths. I am talking about changing the nature of the penis or the phallus, so that it will never again be conceived of or used as a weapon; transforming the signs of masculinity into emblems of sexual prowess, protectiveness, and the strength of a hero instead of markers worn by a predator.

It was a transcendental experience, watching mustaches grind together, male tongue in male mouth, man hand in man butt, dicks rubbing together in various stages of erection. It was transforming for me, and I don't think I have ever stopped trying to understand it or communicate some of the implications of how I felt at that moment. I grew up in a very crazy fundamentalist christian family where there were many layers of homophobia. When you want to write about your experience as a queer person you need to always be aware of the negative messages we've heard about homosexuality all our lives. Because this body of defeatist and hateful mythology separates us from our own experience. These complex layers of homophobia make it hard for us to see ourselves, which is what we have to do before we can write with accuracy or insight.

The first layer of homophobia is that queers don't exist, that homosexuals are such a tiny group of people that we're simply nowhere at all. This sort of antigay message is spread by not putting gay characters in prime-time television shows, keeping gay books out of libraries, making it very dangerous for gay and bisexual men and women to come out of the closet, and all the other things that straight people do to keep us invisible. Because they are very visibly different, it's sexual minority queers—for example, the effeminate men and the butch dykes in leather jackets—who combat this type of homophobia every day, simply by taking a bus or getting a job. The most successful tactic the straight majority uses on this level is to convince us that we need to remain hidden in order to guarantee our own safety. Then we patrol our own borders and contain or punish any member of our community who becomes "too obvious." No one knows better than members of a minority how to police their own.

Underneath that is the second layer of homophobia, which says that what we do is disgusting and revolting and it makes people sick. Being unmentionable is a slight improvement over being invisible. It's nudging a little closer to public view. This is where some of the most painful voices of shame are rooted. I am conscious of hearing these voices every time I sit down to write. It has taken years of work to be able to answer them back and tune them out. I think what we need to remember as queer writers when we confront this ugliness is that there is a piece of homophobia that is about straight envy of gay sexual license. Our erotic natures have been described to us by people who cannot deal with their own pleasures. Heterosexuals have a lot of work to do on themselves before they have much room to criticize fags and dykes. They should be thinking about and talking about teen pregnancy, venereal disease, overpopulation, domestic violence, and female inorgasmia before they rant about our stuff. Nor can we buy off our persecutors by reining in our erotic abandon.

The third layer of queer hatred says same-sex activity is ridiculous, a parody of heterosexuality, an awkward attempt to achieve pleasure that will forever elude us because our bodies don't fit together. Does anybody but me remember Dr. David Reuben's 1969 opus *Everything You Always Wanted to Know About Sex* (*But Were Afraid to Ask)* with its awful dictum, "Just as one penis plus one penis equals nothing, one vagina plus another vagina still equals zero"? Before I ever licked a clit, I knew that had to be bullshit. So much happens when two women simply sit next to each other and hold hands! The very air between them fills up with the color of potential intimacy. I got one five-minute close-dancing lesson from another girl in junior high school, and the smell of her hairspray and the feel of our breasts rubbing against each other was enough lesbian sex to get me through the next five years of no contact at all with other female bodies. But what can we expect from a group of people who, by and large, cannot deal with the revolutionary things they could experience during vanilla penis-in-vagina sex? It seems to me that heterosexual culture has devoted a great deal of energy to guaranteeing that a penis plus a vagina will always equal zero—no social change, no insight, no shared understanding, and above all, no switching of intimate apparel.

When you get closer to the heart of the onion of homohatred, if you can still see it through all the tears that you've shed to get that far, what you'll discover is this other piece of reverse homophobia that says, actually, queer sex is so amazing, it's addicting, and if you get some it will spoil you for anything else. This was a popular theme in lesbian pulps during the '50s. Now, that is where we start to come closer to the truth. It's not that being fucked in the ass will break something inside a man so he can't satisfy a woman, or that a lesbian's tongue is so abnormally long and agile that it will turn any straight girl into a pervert. What's addicting about gay sexuality is its honesty: the willingness we have, as queers, to face the truth of our own fantasies and desires, and choose to own them and follow them, even if we face horrendous penalties. This is what we have to offer straight people who want to be our allies—our courageous dedication to our own notions of passion. We are not the only group of people dealing with a heritage of sexual shame and repression. Heterosexuals really need our help and inspiration, and I wish they'd admit it.

When I first saw men having sex with each other it confronted every single layer of homophobia in a direct and visceral way. Bathhouses and sex clubs remain the target of conservatives, both gay and straight, in part because their very existence demonstrates that much of the denial of homosexual desire is false. If you're in the middle of a club occupied by several hundred men who are all attacking each other's bodies, it becomes very clear that we do exist, in great numbers, and that our desire for each other is in fact a very powerful thing.

Speaking of bathhouses brings me to another factor that pulled me toward writing in a male persona. Gay men have got institutions and traditions that allow them to be sexually adventurous in ways that women usually are not. When I was trying to create a life for myself as a sexually adventurous woman, I wanted to see what I could find in those traditions that might be useful for me and other women. I also wanted to know how I limited myself. I wanted to know what assumptions I made about what was possible and what was not possible that kept what felt like a big cast iron lid on my libido. I loved the fact that men would walk into bars, grab each others' nipples, and pat each other on the crotch. They could have this ten-second conversation and then go off and fuck. I didn't know any women who could do that. You wouldn't get that far with a girl if you bought her dinner for six weeks in a row! Fortunately, things have changed a lot in lesbian culture. Cross-pollination is a good thing.

As a visible S/M dyke, I know about my own oppression. I've lived with it every single day of my life. But I never wanted to stop there. The oppression of women and dykes is part of a larger system, and I want to know how the whole thing works. I want to know what it does to us on a personal level and on a cultural level, and how we can escape. Or, if we cannot muster the strength to overcome our jailers, at least we can know the contours of our prison. Writing about sexuality should do all of these things: document the damage, celebrate our resistance, and point toward a future where we are untrammeled.

For example, there are important differences between the oppression of little boy fags and little girl dykes. It's difficult to generalize, but I believe gay men have been damaged in some ways that lesbians have not. By trying to describe these differences, I do not mean to downplay the vicious and unconscionable things that are done to young women to try to eliminate lesbianism. But when we assume that the coming-out process of a gay man mirrors that of a lesbian, we set ourselves up to have some deep misunderstandings.

Lesbian invisibility (a part of the general repression and denial of women's sexuality) makes most adults a great deal more vigilant about the sexuality and masculinity of little boys than they are of little girls' identities. A little boy who plays with girls' toys, or girls themselves, and does not feature boorish butch behavior, is always going to be labeled a sissy, a fag in the making. A butch little girl is called a tomboy, or, when she gets older, any of the epithets applied in this culture to unattractive women. She is more likely to be seen as a poor excuse for a heterosexual than a dyke. While both boys and girls are liable to be physically abused, our culture gives parents more permission to beat up little boys, under the guise of "making men out of them." A young gay man is perceived as actively rejecting a privileged role in the patriarchy. He is typically singled out for more abuse and more punitive treatment than a girl who can hide behind the label of "wallflower" or "jock."

Because of the aforementioned lesbian invisibility, it takes many young lesbians longer to figure out who they are than adolescent gay men. Lesbians frequently get sidetracked by body image issues. It's easier to give in to mandatory heterosexuality when the culture tells you sex isn't supposed to be much fun for women anyway. A woman can pass as heterosexual by just remaining passive; it's not that easy for a gay man to fake a heterosexual response.

Some of the differences between gay male and lesbian culture come from this differential treatment from the larger culture. Gay men are often focused on obtaining sexual pleasure without being limited or punished, and they want the same financial perks that their straight brothers have, if only to prove they have not been "ruined" by being homosexual. Lesbian sexual iconography is so much broader than gay male pornography because most of us are fighting the damage done by years of being told we were ugly and physically repulsive.

These differences make it hard to talk to one another in real life, and when you write fiction for these two very different groups of readers, you have to take them into account. It also changes the definition of what's subversive. Getting a gay man to jack off to a story about a disabled man or an old man or a fat man means something very different, for example, than writing similar stories for a lesbian audience.

These differences, and others I don't have the space to describe here, are the original reasons for the construction of what is now called "identity politics." It's important to remember how costly it could be to come out of the closet simply as a feminist, much less a queer, back in the '50s and '60s. The punishment for the tiniest infractions of social sex-roles or sexual mores were draconian. Among the people who were working for social change, either out of conviction, or because there was something about them which made it impossible for them to hide and conform, or both, there was a conviction that if you could find enough people of your own kind, you could also be sure you were among like-minded people you could trust, people with whom you could share a political agenda. It was a utopian vision of finally achieving safety; an end to bitter and frightening loneliness.

In some ways, the repudiation of identity politics that's so popular today is a luxury, made possible by the formation of relatively large communities of gay, bisexual, and transgendered people. While we are still penalized for being different, the harshness of those punishments has been ameliorated somewhat by the fact that we now have enough numbers to look more like cohesive, well-organized minority groups and less like one weird kid all alone on the playground. Unfortunately, the cohesiveness is an optical illusion produced by viewing us from a distance through the lens of heterosexual privilege. We have learned, over decades of painful struggle, just how divisive, untrustworthy, partisan, petty, and selfish the people who share our deviance can be.

Eschewal of identity politics was an inevitable side-effect of achieving some partial success and building aboveground organizations and neighborhoods of our own. As it became slightly less costly to be known as "queer," whatever you think that means, more and more people affiliated with deviant communities of one sort or another, and with them they brought a diversity of political agendas. As gay identity became more visible, it also became more diffuse. Politically active bisexuals and transgendered people are not upstarts trying to hitch a ride on the coattails of lesbian and gay freedom. These "newer" sexual minorities have always been present, but they are now reaching enough critical mass of their own to individuate, name themselves, and agitate for their own liberation. They are the inevitable and logical next generation, living testament to the success of older subcultures, and it would be a great shame if they were disowned by their ancestors.

Unfortunately, certain segments of the gay male and lesbian communities have already taken steps to distance themselves from bisexuals, transgendered people, sadomasochists, and anybody else who doesn't fit into assimilationist politics. Other than their unsuitability for mainstreaming, there are other reasons for rejecting these bastard children. Bisexuals blur the clear boundaries that separate gays from straights, us from them, the good and oppressed people from the enemy. Transgendered people blur the boundaries between women and men, with similar consequences. And S/M people challenge the whole idea that sexual orientation ought to be based on gender in the first place, since many of us care more about the fetishistic aspects of our partners' apparel or the equipment they are prepared to wield than we do about the contents of their laps.

While a battle between us and them, good and evil, is easy to write speeches about and fab for recruitment posters, it may not be an accurate reflection of how and why some groups in our society are singled out for privilege and others for second-class status. Especially evil people can always be found within government or the private sector who make good targets for caricature and civil disobedience. But simply replacing those people with more liberal individuals does not seem to uproot homophobia, misogyny, sexism, racism, etc. While key people do assume responsibility, at specific historical moments, for grinding the disenfranchised beneath their heels, in general our mistreatment is more diffuse, hard to locate, elusive, and therefore difficult to eliminate.

So movements for social change have increasingly formed around specific agendas, rather than around identities. To some extent, the existence of ACT-UP and Queer Nation exemplifies this historical shift. Although gay men with AIDS were the backbone and ballast of these organizations, they were also infused with the energy of radical lesbians and other people who were simply angry about the way government, the medical industry, and pharmaceutical companies were fucking up their response to the epidemic and murdering us with their indifference and incompetence.

An identity-driven movement for social change is effective at creating public space and a political voice for a given minority. But such movements also get bogged down by internecine warfare over what the parameters of that identity should be, who gets to enforce the parameters, and what should happen to those who disobey. The so-called "feminist sex wars" of the '80s are a great example of this kind of wasteful civil war. The tendency to organize new movements around agreement with concrete political goals, rather than the possession of a persecuted (and therefore politically privileged) identity, is an attempt to avoid these costly and debilitating battles.

Identity-based movements became obsolete the moment we realized that we cannot expect to overcome our opposition by recruiting them. Gay male activists of the '70s were often guilty of assuming that there was no such thing as a heterosexual man. Any guy you blew was a feather in your political cap—as if that was enough to get him to show up at the next Gay Freedom Day Parade, or riot when Dan White got acquitted. Early lesbian feminists had a similar sense of pride and confidence about seducing ostensibly "straight" women into a lifestyle that promised better sex and a harmonious relationship with an equal. (Ha!) Making allies outside our beleaguered spheres is a more practical approach, and our success at doing this also undermines the hegemony of identity politics.

Agenda-based attempts to shift the majority's notions of proper sexual or gender boundaries can expect to be successful unless oppression sharply increases. I predict that if the penalties for being sexually deviant or feminist become much more harsh, alliances based on political agreement will falter. Most people would rather put their principles aside than face a higher probability of street violence, incarceration in a mental institution, a prison sentence, or permanent unemployment—all things that you could expect if you were a queer or a Communist for much of the '50s and '60s. Under systematic and intense government suppression, I would once again expect most opponents of the sex-and-gender system to be fanatic idealists or those who have to fight back because there is no way for them to blend in or pass as "normal." Under such social conditions, persecution once more would assume the character of being managed by specific highly visible enemies and institutions, so the us/them dichotomy would be in force again.

Unfortunately, I expect the pendulum to swing back in a more repressive direction, despite any gains made by agenda-dominated movements for social change, if such efforts focus on behavior rather than attitudes. When drawing up a list of things to attack, it is much easier to focus on concrete laws, social policies, and religious precepts than it is to attack the complex web of psychological and spiritual shortcomings that spawn discrimination and stigma. Proposition 209 recently passed in California, wiping out decades of affirmative action programs which had barely begun to address gender and racial inequalities. This is the sort of failure I am talking about. Determined and sincere attempts to wipe out racism by legislating against it will be vulnerable to backlash as long as most white people believe that racial minorities are inferior people who require preferential treatment in order to "compete" with whites for jobs and educational opportunities. Progressive organizations need to develop sophisticated analyses that will allow them to address and alleviate the resentment that inevitably accompanies any gains made by a sexual or racial minority. Unfortunately, this is hard to do in a gay and lesbian movement dominated by a capitalist ideology, because this resentment is often the product of economic insecurity which victimizes even relatively privileged Caucasian working people. Movements for sexual liberation can no longer afford to ignore class issues.

In the meantime, the reader of this article could be excused if he, she, or shim wondered what all this had to do with identity sedition in pornography. So let me close with the notion that pleasure which crosses the boundaries of identity challenges those limitations. There are dykes who jack off to *Drummer* magazine or vanilla all-boy porn; gay men who jack off to *On Our Backs* or *Macho Sluts;* bisexual porn which invites everyone to catch a fast ride to gratification; transsexual or transvestite porn which invites you to think of yourself as a different gender, or neither. Some of us jump the fence and play in one another's id-filled wading pools. So how alien can we really be to one another? I don't think a shared sense of the erotic necessarily creates a shared political agenda, but it certainly facilitates it. And I'm not trying to make anyone whose choice of porn is consistent with their self-label feel inferior. I wouldn't want the possibility of pansexuality to become tyrannical.

I just wonder if some of the sense we all have, as members of our own little box, that we are special and different and uniquely good, is not simply a reaction to being told so often that we are terrible and awful and wrong. My own life has been a lot richer and more genuine for climbing out of the box of lesbian-feminist-leather-dyke. One of the nasty things that happens in ghettos is the way that we repress and punish one another just because we can. Because we're in a cell, we're like lobsters in a lobster tank. We have access to each other and we don't have access to the people who put us there. But we can beat each other up and make each other feel bad if we don't conform to the rigid rules of our tiny little community. I don't want to live in a ghetto, not as a pervert, not as a lesbian, not as a writer. I live in the whole world.

We get afraid to raise our heads. We get afraid to look outside of the walls that we've built to try to protect ourselves from persecution. And I think that it is important that we do raise our heads and put down on the page whatever it is that we see.

This essay is based in part on remarks delivered at "Switch Hitters," a panel about men who write lesbian porn and women who write gay male porn, held as part of A Different Light's Readers and Writers Conference in April of 1996. Thanks are due to Val Langmuir for her extensive editorial assistance.

HER BODY, MINE, AND HIS

DOROTHY ALLISON

Frog fucking. Her hands on my hips; my heels against my ass, legs spread wide; her face leaning into my neck; my hands gripping her forearms. Her teeth are gentle. Nothing else about her is. I push up on the balls of my feet, rock my ass onto my ankles, reaching up for every forward movement of her thighs between mine. Her nipples are hard, her face flushed, feet planted on the floor while I arch off the edge of the bed, a water mammal, a frog creature with thighs snapping back to meet her every thrust.

My labia swell. I can feel each hair that curls around the harness she wears. I imagine manta rays unfolding great undulating labia-wings in the ocean, wrapping around the object of their desire. Just so my labia, the wings of my cunt. I reach for her with my hands, my mouth, my thighs, my great swollen powerful cunt.

Her teeth are set, hips are thrusting, shoving, head back, pushing, drawing back and ramming in. I laugh and arch up into her, curse her, beg her. My feet are planted. I can do anything. I lift my belly, push up even more. Fucking, fucking, fucking. I call this fucking. Call her lover, bastard, honey, sweetheart, nasty motherfucker, evil-hearted bitch, YOU GOD-DAMNED CUNT! She calls me her baby, her girl, her toy, her lover, hers, hers, hers. Tells me she will never stop, never let me go. I beg her. "Fuck me. Hard." I beg her. "You, you, you…hard! Goddamn you! Do it! Don't stop! Don't stop! Don't stop! Don't stop!"

Jesus fucking christ don't stop.

Don't stop.

I have been told that lesbians don't do this. Perhaps we are not lesbians? She is a woman. I am a woman. But maybe we are aliens? Is what we do together a lesbian act?

Paul took me out for coffee in New York and gave me a little silver claw holding a stone. "A little something for that poem of yours," he told me. "The one about the joy of faggots. I've been reading it everywhere." He drank herbal tea and told me about his travels, reading poetry and flirting with the tender young boys at all the universities, going on about how they kneel in the front row and look up to him, their lips gently parted and their legs pressed together. Sipping tea he told me, "They're wearing those loose trousers again, the ones with the pleats that always remind me of F. Scott Fitzgerald and lawn parties."

I drank bitter coffee, admired his narrow mustache, and told him how much I hate those blouson pants women are wearing instead of jeans. "It's hell being an ass woman these days," I joked.

He started to laugh, called me a lech, looked away, looked back, and I saw there were tears in his eyes. Said, "Yes, those jeans, tight, shaped to the ass, worn to a pale blue-white and torn, like as not showing an ass-cheek paler still." Said, "Yes, all those boys, those years, all the men in tight-tight pants." Said, "Yes, those jeans, the pants so tight their cocks were clearly visible on the bus, the subway, the street, a shadow of a dick leading me on. Sometimes I would just lightly brush them, and watch them swell under the denim, the dick lengthening down the thigh." He stopped, tears all over his face, his hand on his cup shaking, coming up in the air to gesture. A profound sad movement of loss. "All gone," he whispered, the romantic poet in his suede professor's jacket. "I never do it anymore, never. Never touch them, those boys. Can't even imagine falling in love again, certainly not like I used to for twenty minutes at a time on any afternoon."

I started to speak, but he put his hand up. "Don't say it. Don't tell me I'm being foolish or cowardly or stupid or anything. I loved the way it used to be and I hate the fact that it's gone. I've not become celibate, or silly, or vicious, or gotten religion, or started lecturing people in bars. It's those memories I miss, those boys on the street in the afternoon laughing and loving each other, that sense of sex as an adventure, a holy act."

He put his cup down, glared at it and then at me. Indignant, excited, determined. "But you still do it, don't you? You dykes! You're out there all the time doing it. Flirting with each other, touching, teasing, jerking each other off in bathrooms, picking each other up and going to parties. Fucking and showing off and doing it everywhere you can. You are. Say you are. I know you are."

I said, "Yes." I lied and said, "Yes, Paul, we are. Yes."

She has named her cock Bubba. Teases me with it. Calls it him, says, "Talk to him, pet him. He's gonna go deep inside you." I start to giggle, slap Bubba back and forth. Cannot take this too seriously, even though I really do like it when she straps him on. Bubba is fat and bent, an ugly pink color not found in nature, and he jiggles obscenely when she walks around the room. Obscene and ridiculous, still he is no less effective when she puts herself between my legs. Holding Bubba in one hand I am sure that this is the origin of irony—that men's penises should look so funny and still be so prized.

She is ten years younger than me...sometimes. Sometimes I am eight and she is not born yet, but the ghost of her puts a hand on my throat, pinches my clit, bites my breast. The ghost of her teases me, tells me how much she loves all my perversities. She says she was made for me, promises me sincerely that she will always want me. Sometimes I believe her without effort. Sometimes I become her child, trusting, taking in everything she says. Her flesh, her body, her lust and hunger—I believe. I believe, and it is not a lie.

When I am fucking her I am a thousand years old, a crone with teeth, bone teeth grinding, vibrating down into my own hips. Old and mean and hungry as a wolf, or a shark. She is a suckling infant, soft in my hands, trusting me with her tender open places. Her mouth parts like an oyster, the lower lip soft under the tongue, the teeth pearls in the dim light. Her eyes are deep and dark and secret. She is pink, rose, red, going purple dark…coming with a cry and a shudder, and suddenly limp beneath my arms. I push up off her and bite my own wrist. It is all I can do not to feed at her throat.

I drank too much wine at a party last fall, found myself quoting Muriel Rukeyser to Geoff Mains, all about the backside, the body's ghetto, singing her words, "Never to go despising the asshole nor the useful shit that is our clean clue to what we need."

"The clitoris in her least speech," he said back, and I loved him for that with all my soul. We fed each other fat baby carrots and beamed at our own enjoyment.

"Ah, the ass," Geoff intoned, "the temple of the gods."

I giggled, lifted a carrot in a toast, matched his tone. "And the sphincter—gateway to the heart."

He nodded, licked his carrot, reached down, shifted a strap, and inserted that carrot deftly up his butt. He looked up at me, grinned, rolled a carrot in my direction, raised one eyebrow. "Least speech," I heard myself tell him. Then I hiked up my skirt and disappeared the carrot, keeping my eyes on his all the while. There was something about his expression, a look of arrogant conviction that I could not resist.

"Lesbians constantly surprise me," was all Geoff said, lining up a row of little baby carrots from the onion dip to the chips, pulling the dish of butter over as well. He handed me another carrot. I blinked, then watched as he took one for himself. "I propose the carrot olympics, a cross-gender, mutually queer event," he challenged. I started to laugh as he rolled buttery carrots between his palms. His face was full of laughter, his eyes so blue and pleased with himself they sparkled.

"All right," I agreed. How could I not? I pulled up the hem of my skirt, tucked it into my waistband, took up the butter, and looked Geoff right in the eye. "Dead heat, or one on one?"

FAGGOT! That's what he called me. The boy on the street with the baseball bat who followed me home from Dolores Park the week after I moved to San Francisco. HE called me a faggot. My hair is long. My hips are wide. I wear a leather jacket and walk with a limp. But I carry a knife. What am I exactly? When he called me a faggot I knew. I knew for sure who I was and who I would not be. From the doorway of a grocery at 18th and Guerrero I yelled it at him. "Dyke! Get it right, you son-of-a-bitch, I'm a dyke."

I am angry all the time lately, and being angry makes me horny, makes me itchy, makes me want to shock strangers and surprise the girls who ask me, please, out for coffee and to talk. I don't want to talk. I want to wrestle in silence. It isn't sex I want when I am like this. It's the intimacy of their bodies, the inside of them, what they are afraid I might see if I look too close. I look too close. I write it all down. I intend that things shall be different in my lifetime, if not in theirs.

Paul, Geoff—I am doing it as much as I can, as fast as I can. This holy act. I am licking their necks on Market Street, fisting them in the second floor bathroom at Amelia's, in a booth under a dim wall lamp at the Box—coming up from her cunt a moment before the spotlight shifts to her greedy features. I have her tied to a rail in a garage down on Howard Street, let her giggle and squirm while I teased her clit, then filled her mouth with my sticky fingers and rocked her on my hipbone till she roared. We have roared together. Everywhere I go, the slippery scent of sweat and heat is in the air, so strong it could be me or the women I follow, the ones who follow me. They know who I am just as I know them. I have ripped open their jeans at the Powerhouse, put my heel between their legs at the Broadway Café, opened their shirts all the way down at Just Desserts, and pushed seedless grapes into their panties at the Patio Café. The holy act of sex, my sex, done in your name, done for the only, the best reason. Because we want it.

I am pushing up off the bed into Alix's neck like a great cat with a gazelle in her teeth. I am screaming and not stopping, not stopping. Frog fucking, pussy creaming, ass clenching, drumming out, pumping in. I am doing it, boys and girls, I am doing it, doing it all the time.

HERMAPHRODYKES:
GIRLS WILL BE BOYS AND DYKES WILL BE FAGS

If queer women have shown increasing regard for gay men, it's hardly surprising that some have wanted to adopt the very sexual possibilities queer men represent to them. So it has been that in one of the strange twists of postmodern sexual culture, just as scores of gay men have "gone lesbian" and retreated to the emotional and hopefully physical safety of monogamous partnerings, scores of queer women have "gone fag," constructing male personas, daddy/boy (or daddy/girl) relationships, and women's sex clubs on the ashes of the bath-house era. For women raised to be good girls it's a walk on the wild side; for girls who grew up under feminism, it's a way of taking postmodern queer theory to the streets.

Do queer men hide secret lesbian personas? Probably not as commonly as queer women are going fag. We know straight men fantasize about lesbians in droves (with the presumption being that, at some point, he will enter the scene and satisfy both women in a display of his overwhelming masculine virility and prowess), but there seems to be no queer male sexual or literary movement to compare to the advent of the "girlfags."

Here, Laura Antoniou reveals the journey, fraught with both pain and healing, she underwent in claiming her identity as a "Boy," whereas Jill Nagle aggressively stalks a place for herself in the "Men's Room."

ANTI-VENOM FOR THE SOUL
(PLUS CONVERSATIONS I NEVER REALLY HAD)

LAURA ANTONIOU

There would come a moment, when the silences punctuating the discussion would stretch to two, three, five, ten seconds. When the postures would relax and tense up—one leaning back, the other arching forward. I'd know when it was time, and I'd excuse myself to the bathroom, ostensibly for its mundane use. There, I'd take off my bra, adjust the harness tight between my legs. There, I'd struggle to shed my body, my self-image, my entire gender identity, so that I could walk out, my cock hard against my thigh, my nuts aching, ready.

It rarely worked. I'm no slender androgyne, with tits small enough to bind or even leave free. My tits and hips and ass are wide and soft, my belly full—no washboard abs or long legs. My face is soft and rounded, eyes large and framed by ridiculously thick lashes. No human being on the planet would mistake that form for male.

No, I'm not a guy. That piece of silicone between my legs will never feel piss or cum shooting through it. I will never actually feel the tenderness and ecstasy of a hand on its shaft, at its base, the sensuous flicking of a tongue at its tip. I do not believe in my own prick.

Until his hand was upon it.

Then, I believed. Close enough, so they say, for jazz.

"That's my daughter who wants to be a boy," the man who married my mother said more than once. I repeat it these days to knowledgeable friends, understanding strangers, my voice heavy with the irony of his prescience. How little he knew, I laugh. I can laugh now. I grew up and, indeed, I became a boy.

And it was every bit as interesting and liberating as I thought it would be. It was also more challenging than I could have ever imagined. It has left me with a burden of tales untold. Until now.

I had been living and traveling in a world full of dykes, almost every one of them butch as can be. I was a little awed in this company, because it was so unlike the way I thought I lived at home. They were so bold and direct, swaggering and strong and tough, and all so handsomely clothed in tight jeans and leather boots. I aspired to be one of them. I didn't yet realize I already was. In our moments of honesty and courage, we exposed ourselves and our wounds to each other and found that a remarkable percentage of us had suffered at the hands of adult men in our lives and families.
We said:
> "If I had been a boy, he would have
> just hit me
> just yelled at me
> been proud of me
> loved me
> not noticed me
> left me alone."

Someone said: "All women are really looking for father figures."

Of course I was disturbed by the neo-Freudian implications of what we (I) were (was) doing, who we (I) were (was) pretending to be. My fuzzy Psych 101 theorizing left me with images of women seeking to reenact episodes of abuse and injustice, pain and humiliation. Even as I spiraled deep into a competitive drive for experiences that were more intense, more shattering, more damaging, every shift came with the struggle to get beyond what seemed so obvious. In order to achieve the sense of danger and intimacy I was driven to, I needed to find a paradigm to adopt, a role that would make it safe for me. Safe to say the words. Safe under a hand.

One night, I was brave enough to say it. "I want to be a boy," I said. "Actually, I think I am one."

This story would be almost commonplace if it happened on the West Coast, and the person I said it to was another dyke, and everyone reading this was into leather and knew what a Daddy/Boy relationship was.

Naturally, I live on the East Coast, and the person I said it to was a bisexual man, and most of the people we knew were into D/S and S/M, not "leather," and if they could be made to understand the "Daddy" part, there was simply no explaining the "Boy" part.

"And you're his little girl," one thoroughly heterosexual man said brightly and kindly, after hearing that my chosen top was my Daddy. He was so pleased with his reasoning skills. He didn't know why I never liked him, couldn't give him the time of day.

Fact was, what he suggested disgusted me. I'm no man's little girl. I never was.

It felt like the right thing to do, to me. It was a way for me to enact the fantasy life I dreamed about, to engage in a relationship with a man that had limits and boundaries, yet went so much deeper than a friendly, casual fuck-buddy arrangement. It gave me a chance to co-create a relationship that was both nurturing and authority-laden, forward thinking and traditional. It gave me a chance to try again, to have that special kind of relationship that we imagine could/should exist between a parent-like adult mentor and their junior partner, a person learning through emulation and reward and punishment scenarios. But consider the ample contradictions inherent in the situation—a dyke, woman-identified abuse survivor with an older, not purely gay-identified man doing S/M in an intimate and publicly acknowledged relationship.

It cost me dearly. Not only in the various ways I was made to feel unwelcome in parts of the lesbian leather community, and also feel odd in the mixed/hetero S/M scene, but by being in one of those places that defied conventional use of language.

As a writer, I am very concerned with language. When I say I'm a dyke, I mean dyke, not lesbian, not female homosexual, not gay woman. I was never one of those people who say, "I don't believe in labels, they're so limiting," as though not believing in something makes it go away. Labels are vital in our culture; they provide instant identification, associative reasoning fodder, and a base from which to move on. Adopting the paradigm title of "Boy" meant taking on all the gay male cultural implications of the role, plus examining the identity of the masculine, period. It also meant examining my deepest fears and my terrible self-image. It took me to the core of my identity—dyke/woman—and shook it repeatedly as I wondered what it all meant.

Someone said, "How can you call yourself a dyke? Dykes are like super lesbians. If you have sex with men, you're not a lesbian at all. You're bisexual."

I once identified as a bisexual woman. I took that to mean that I had a more or less equal chance of establishing a relationship with a man or a woman. That almost all of my male partners were queer themselves didn't really sink in until years later, when I discovered that every other lesbian on the planet had not grown up fantasizing about and having sex only with girls. I dropped that label when I realized that, really, I would never want to actually share all of my life with a man. No matter how fine they looked, how well they played or fucked, or how friendly I was with them, they would never feel right in my bed, night after night. I dreamed of women. I was a dyke.

To settle into feeling, breathing, living as a dyke, and then find that I was drawn to a man—a big, hairy, thoroughly masculine man, who was not the safe, sexy, but ultimately untouchable gay leather daddy who I could flirt with, act with, and never actually do anything sexual with—was a surprise, to say the least.

To be drawn to him at the same time that my mind was entertaining such complicated puzzles as my core identity and the meaning behind my fantasies, was pure luck. When we were flirting and getting to know each other, neither one of us could have seen what was ahead. Perhaps we both would have shied away if we had. How glorious that we didn't.

Someone said, "This is a lesbian woman's event. Bisexuals only bring male energy to this space, and taint it. We need a space to be safe among our own kind."

"Then you're saying," I repeated, a moment away from tears of betrayal, staring strong, staying calm, keeping myself proud and composed, "that I am not welcome to return."

To my face, she said, "Yes."

I went back anyway, and never hid my past, my tastes, my relationships, my fantasies and life choices. And I would hide my tangled feelings of exposure and hurt and, yes, shame, and I never let them know how I felt in reaction to what they said, what they suggested. Each time I walked across new thresholds and felt the sickening terror that comes with being uncloseted and accessible. Each time I waited for the next confrontation, the next time a woman used the power of womanspace to attempt to segregate me, to negate me. Perhaps I should have let them know. Perhaps I should have cried a woman's tears of frustration and pain and anger and made them see how their defense of turf was actually hurting another woman. But I was too proud. I went back and let them see my calm strength, and occasionally my anger. After a while, it wasn't considered as important. Or perhaps my increasing notoriety as an author and editor overcame the distaste some women felt for my sexual (and emotional) proclivities. Or, maybe it was because more women began to admit that they, too, had S/M relationships with men. But I knew I was still different. My particular man was known to be bisexual. By extension and logic, so, therefore, was I.

Someone said, "If two queers are having sex with each other, it's still queer sex."

People ask me now, were we fags together? In other words, did I pretend to be a gay man, while he pretended to be a gay man, and then we could both play happily in a world of make-believe?

Yes, it was like that exactly, and no, it wasn't like that at all.

I wore a dick, but it never shot cum. I took my bra off, but never hid my big tits. I never changed my name, never adopted a "boy name" like I hear others did, and there was never the slightest attempt to alter pronoun usage with me. "She's my boy," was always a conversational grenade, guaranteed to cause an immediate reaction. Tossed into a circle of people, it would hurl semantic shrapnel into the dialogue as people grappled with what it meant.

The struggle with my core identity never even approached the level of suspension of disbelief necessary for the sort of method acting that I would have to do to pretend I was a young man, pretend that I was raised as a boy, that my body was built on a masculine frame. For me, gender role was only a part of the attraction, and eventually not even of central importance. It was the definition of the role beyond gender or orientation. A boy was potential and glory, a bearer of pride and attention and strict, loving affection. A romantic ideal with real-world models in every corner of literature, myth, and folklore, modern culture.

A boy was expected to grow up.

And it was so necessary that I had the room to grow the fuck up.

How I needed that structure, that framework for survival! Years of playing at doing S/M had provided me with some measure of skill, some level of expertise, but my passion for order and stability was never sated for long. Having found a pattern to lay down and follow, I needed to complete that leg of the journey, to go from start to finish in an honorable way, to experience the pain and joy with all the energy my long-closeted fantasies could generate. I needed to sink myself into it. So, yes, we were fags together, and we were also a man and a woman acting out a complex, deep-seated romantic fantasy which neither one of us could have predicted or entirely controlled.

Someone said, "It's okay as long as you never have sex with him. That would be unhealthy, dangerous, sick."

Entering into this relationship created a whole new way for sex to become complicated. Was it sexual to be beaten, or disciplined? Sexual to endure pain, or teasing, or bondage for its own sake? Or is it what people really wanted to know: Did I suck his cock? Did we screw? If he fucked me, exactly how did it occur? What combinations of genitalia and bodily fluids were encountered, and how often?

And the complications weren't only in the direct and personally demanding way these things were asked of me (and yes, people did ask me), but in the knee-jerk way I felt almost compelled to answer them. Fighting off defensiveness was always a part of my struggle, striving to balance the righteousness of my own passion with the enduring discomfort I seemed to cause in others. Even now, years later, I wonder if it is necessary to say something, if it's part of this story or not. After all, I don't ask other people about the details of their sexual lives; I take their word that they are what they say they are, and leave any theories about how exactly they act on their identity to idle and private musings. And then, only if I really care to wonder.

But how could our relationship not be about sex, and sexual acts? I don't do these things strictly for mental jollies, my body is as hungry as anyone else's. When a voice or an action or a touch turns me on, it's my cunt that responds and gets wet, it's my large and very unmasculine nipples that get hard. Sure, my metaphoric dick gets hard, but when I come, it's going to be via my clit, no matter what the circumstances were that made me ready for it. So, hell yes, it was a sexual thing.

But what did you do? I still hear the voices asking, insisting. Did he ever fuck you? Was it the queer sex that we imagine? Was it a reenactment of your past abuse? Was it just another example of patriarchal violence against women, perpetrated with the woman's pseudo-consent? Was it good, did you come? Did he? Where? How?

None of your fucking business.

He was my Daddy.

I was his Boy.

The rest is personal.

Someone said, "I see you've gone back to being a lesbian now."

I never left. I didn't even take a vacation. I never stopped loving women, lusting after women, wanting women. I never doubted that my primary partner would once again be a woman. Just as I never really became a boychild, so I never really became authentically bisexual, let alone straight. Yet still, I find it difficult to talk about that time, nearly impossible to write about it. Who can I tell this story to, the tale of a soul that was injected with the poison of a toxic childhood and adolescence, but which found solace in the melodramatic mimicking of a parent-child relationship? Where could there be a place to talk about the challenges and rewards of not-being-het? I could pour it out into a novel maybe, but every time I try it comes out raw and rough, as though I was discovering a new form of storytelling. I need to wrestle with the language, almost physically wring meaning from the words one at a time, stopping to define and redefine at every step. It's torturous, and clumsy. It doesn't suffice. It doesn't do that time, that place, or those two people, any justice.

But it's a story that has to be told.

STROKING MY INNER FAG

JILL NAGLE

Avi and I made the perfect couple for the Faerie Lingerie Soiree: he wore a lace garter belt with white stockings, cotton bikinis, and my expert make-up job, and I boy Calvin drawers, tank top, butchaline suede vest, matching boots, and faux facial hair. Oh, yes, and the pretty package between my legs.

"How do you guys walk with these things?" I whined.

"Just leave it alone!" admonished Avi in his Israeli falsetto. I tried to saunter casually down the street, tried to give up control of holding my dick in place to the higher power of the black lace g-string in which it was securely nestled.

After several blocks of awkward posturing, and more than one stop to adjust my new jewels, we arrived on the scene. As I expected, the hallways and rooms were full of mostly radical faerie boys in sequins, lace, polyester, and all other manner of lingerie. I hoped I was within the dress code.

Under strict instructions not to blow my cover, Avi dutifully introduced me to his boy friends as Ian, the name I came very close to adopting this Rosh Hashanah. I extended my firmest handshake and intoned "hahzit-goin?" in the manliest tenor I could muster. Some bought it temporarily; others, while they saw through my boy drag, were obviously curious.

In past visits to gay male spaces, I've noticed that my female presence tended to cool the otherwise free-flowing male sexual heat. Here, I wanted quite the opposite. I came to incite and partake freely of abundant sexual energy. But who did "I" need to be to pull that off?

"I" had to be something of a trickster. I didn't want to be boxed and dismissed as "female." I belonged in the space marked "BOY'S ROOM." I wanted in; into the clubhouse and into the hothouse and into some juicy boyflesh....

Before too long, I was banging my firm yet flexible dildo against the butt cheeks of a long line of fags eager to get play-fucked, one after the other in the hallway. I could imagine the headlines: "Girl-Boy Gang-Bangs Gaggle of Faeries, Single-handedly." Single-dildoedly? I don't know if they were my toys, or if I was theirs, but everyone seemed to be enjoying the game.

Some days I feel more butch than others, but this scene made me into another animal entirely. I didn't feel like I was performing butch. The biowimmin at the party were mostly sweet, passive, and femme; they lacked the rawness I craved. Had a big bad butch dyke swaggered in the door, my orientation might have suddenly become decidedly more complicated. As it was, I felt clearly like…a transgendered fag.

I remembered two male-to-female transsexuals I knew. One was Joseph, a gay man who, he said, planned to become a lesbian after surgery. Planned? To become a lesbian? What's lesbian, then, if you can schedule becoming one? The other was Kate Bornstein, a former heterosexual man who, once female, found that her attraction to women remained. She ultimately came out as a lesbian. As Kate quoted her mom in her latest play, "So now we talk, me and my son, the lesbian." For Joseph, the overriding factor in determining his orientation was his preference for the gestalt of queerness, which didn't change along with his sex. For Kate, it was the "sex" of those to whom he, and then she, remained attracted that proved most salient.

There is something about Joseph that I resonate with. Dancing with Spectrum, a radical faerie who gyrated his sinewy body toward and against mine with pointed intent, I thought, *I want this man…I want this man as only a man wanting another man can want.* But perhaps I'm acting out internalized heterophobia—the only way I can act on my attraction to men is as another man. No, that's not quite right, it's more like heterosoporifia: boredom rather than fear of things heterosexual. I can smell het men a hundred yards away and they (yawn) just don't float my boat, whereas queer boys wang my wonger just by blinking.

Spectrum had short, dark hair and piercing eyes with eyebrows that arched from way down close to the nose all the way over the forehead pointing back down toward the ears. His eyes were shadowed such that he appeared intent and focused on whatever he was looking at. He held my gaze, dancing ever closer to me; drops of sweat glistened on his neck. Before long, my shirt was off, my plastic penis was attached above the bay window by its suction cup base so it pointed into the room like a flag-pole, and Spectrum and I had traded undergarments. I danced in his tomato-red jockstrap (over my black g-string) while my gray cotton Calvins skimmed over and between the two hard grapefruits of his exquisite ass. The cotton darkened in spots where his sweat seeped through. I retrieved my cock, which looked quite realistic inside Spectrum's jockstrap. Spectrum's eyes got wide, and he danced toward me, smiling. He stared down, then looked up at my face and giggled shyly. Some of the other faeries drifted over to inspect and play with me, as well. But I deflected them in favor of Spectrum.

Spectrum kept his eyes on me while his hips swiveled closer and clos-er to my crotch. I bent my knees and danced to his chest, "accidentally" grazing my nipple across his. I ran my fingers from the back of his neck down to his navel—stopping again at his nipple to administer a rather sharp tweak. Spectrum's body wavered from head to toe like an inch-worm. Hot damn, I thought. I spun him around and pulled his hips hard against my jockstrap-covered erection; I pushed against his ass, covered by my underwear.

This is now beyond any butch bidyke thing I might be trying to do. I'm kind of a lame butch, anyway. My lover Rebecca, on the other hand, is quite a successful butch. When she and I are together in public, most people go "Jill=femme; Reb=butch."

When we saw Monika Treut's interview with Max Valerio, a female-to-male transsexual and former lesbian feminist, something clicked. I finally began to understand, in my gut, what I had only known intellec-tually: butch and femme can be totally independent of gender orientation.

In my case, my inner fag had long been misidentifed as simply femme.

As a butch bidyke, Rebecca has been a good foil for my emerging gender permutations. She once observed that I hardly ever identify myself as a woman, or even show evidence of thinking of myself that way. That struck me as strange since I consider myself so ardently feminist, but I sort of knew what she was saying. I fully understood one night while standing at the mirror blow-drying my hair.

"I don't understand blow-dryers," Rebecca lamented.

"It's aesthetic," I explained, "and you don't pay a lot of attention to aesthetics." Broad categories of queer iconography, yes. Minute aesthetics, no. Yet that in itself could be considered constitutive of a butch dyke aesthetic. Did my being the opposite make me femme? I was about to try to rationalize how the blow-dryer in question provided a good touchstone for the femme-butch divide, but then I looked in the mirror and it hit me.

"I'm a gay man!" I shouted, waving the blow-dryer around excitedly.

"Yes, that's it!" she exclaimed. We studied me. My tailored silk shirts tucked into pleated men's pants. My "men's" shoes. My chiseled features and prominent jawline. My tapered haircut. The relatively thin, muscular, and flat-chested physique I had cultivated. Even my trademark retro pointy glasses screamed high camp. Indeed, it was mostly gay men who stopped me on the street and shrieked, "I *loooove* your *glasses!*"

And then there were the men in my life. Long after Rebecca's tolerance for "male energy" was spent, I would remain, cavorting with my brothers. A fag hag? Not quite. A bidyke with dildo in tow? Closer, but...I wanted to lovingly wrestle my equal in strength to the ground; I wanted to feel our cocks together. Our real cocks, warm and throbbing....

That was what led to me linger after the Faerie Lingerie Soiree. I didn't think I had imagined Spectrum's blatant flirtations with me. And indeed, I was blessed to find Spectrum in my bed later on, guiding him on a special tour of my (his first) pussy. He was surprised, himself, at thirty-three, only ever having kissed one other woman in his life. I made him suck my cock until he was blue in the face, then I pushed him away and made him watch me plunge my cock deep into my wet pussy again and again. Fucking the very fucking of my gender. Fucking myself with my own cock. Writhing in hermaphroditic-fag-wannabe rushes of fuck-me juice fuck and then and then and then....

And then I let him fuck me—with his real, warm eager cock. My favorite kind of dildo!

Getting fucked normally sends me over the edge quicker than anything, but I was in such empathic awe of his being inside his first pussy ever that most of the throbbing I felt was in my jealous dildo—sort of like a phantom limb.

Spectrum and I played for a good long time, saving many more territories than we traversed, both acknowledging that we'd like there to be a "next time."

Whether "next time" materializes or not, I'm still reeling with the joy of finally liberating my inner fag from her/his lonely closet. Rebecca helped midwife my awareness; the faerie party hosted my debut as a transgendered fag; Spectrum stroked me to a full-tilt, throbbing erection in fag-spawned uncharted territory I can only call hothothot. I've had a hard-on ever since.

GENDER PENDING:
DENYING GENDER IMPERATIVES

No challenge to essentialist thinking packs a greater wallop than a transgendered queer. The transgender community's critique of sexual essentialism is much more than skin deep. Even those transsexuals who have always experienced themselves as "trapped in the wrong body" (which can be a deeply essentialist notion) tweak essentialism and the heterosexist assumptions of the shrinks and surgeons who make up the gauntlet a TS must run to have access to her or his new body, when their orientation turns out queer. Deep down, most people who can calmly contemplate gender reassignment in the first place still believe that pre-surgery TSs are queer, and surgery makes them straight. But the ways gender intersects with sexual orientation are so little understood, and so much more diverse than is commonly acknowledged. Sometimes, like transgendered writer and performance artist David Harrison, they both start out and end up queer—for most of the shrink-and-surgeon crowd (not to mention followers of Oprah) the phenomenon of a lesbian who undergoes gender reassignment to become a gay man is just too confusing a stretch.

The option of hormones and surgery notwithstanding, gender is as much a mental and spiritual phenomenon as a physical one, and within the transgender community are many people who reject the pink-and-blue, either/or gender dichotomy fed us by our culture. These shapeshifters and pioneers may identify as either/or, neither/nor, or as members of that elusive third sex the nineteenth-century sex docs briefly imagined homosexuality to be. Given that there are in fact five common chromosomal genders* (blurred into multiple variants because gender, too, like Kinsey's vision of sexual orientation, exists on a continuum), the fact that we're expected to embody only two truncates our gender expression in a way we can't even imagine.

These three writers explore their gender, identities, and orientations: David Harrison gets personal about his experiences with placing (and answering) personal ads, exploring gay sex with his new body; Riki Anne Wilchins explores the overlapping boundaries where her identities meet in an intellectual "love letter" addressed to Joan Nestle; and Michael Thomas Ford uses the Internet to change gender and find a satisfaction in heterosexual male desire that he can't get from gay men.

* We use the term "gender" here (scientists will chide that "sex" is the correct term) to specify things pertaining to male/female/other, not sex acts. In addition to the commonly-recognized XX and XY chromosomal types, XXY, XYY and XO are seen frequently enough to be called "common."

THE PERSONALS

DAVID HARRISON

I had been consistently perceived as male for at least nine months, after a year and a half on hormones, and hadn't had any surgery yet, when I decided it was time to check out sex with my new body and place my first personal ad. I'd been a lesbian for fifteen years before my transition. Now I was coming out of a long-term relationship and finding myself looking at men. It was during my four-and-a-half-year relationship with none other than the lovely Kate Bornstein, who years earlier had undergone her own gender change, that I transitioned. Kate made it safe for me to face my gender issues which had been chasing me for so long. It was the relationship I had wanted all my life and now, almost as a cruel joke, it too was changing. I was starting to be attracted to men.

Kate saw it coming long before I did. She said. "I have a feeling that if you decide to go through with a gender change, you'll want to be with men and not want to be with me." It was one of her biggest fears, and of course I hotly denied the possibility. But gender changes have their own agendas. Although it took me a long time to actually admit it (because it was such a painful realization), I found myself not attracted to her in the way I used to be. I was not able to give her what she needed because I was so self-involved. And her attraction for me had shifted also. The chemistry had literally changed. "Is it the hormones?" people ask. In my opinion they likely play a large role, but more in facilitating the blossoming of the seed that was there in the first place. I'd had a male homoerotic sensibility as a small child. My first sexual fantasies, at age five, were going to bed at night as Paul and George of the Beatles and taking turns fucking each other.

Anyhow, so here I was, shell-shocked coming out of my relationship (not to mention dealing with my own transition), and really needing to explore sex with men. I was horny as hell and after some encouragement from a couple of friends, I made my first foray into the world of the Personals. I started out by answering other people's ads and it was with one of these encounters that I had my first experience as a transsexual man being with a man. It remains one of my best experiences because we had a great verbal rapport, shared interests, and mutual respect, as well as fun in the sack. We still keep in touch.

When I first started out being sexual as David, I had decided that I didn't want my anatomy getting in the way of me feeling pleasure (although I knew I wanted to get top surgery done). I wanted to be sexual and still feel I could be a man—perhaps stretch the definition of what a man is, in other people's minds—instead of conforming my mind and body to fit someone else's idea. So while I still had breasts, I wore a T-shirt during sex, so I didn't experience dysphoria by being visually reminded of their presence. Different men dealt with me in different ways depending on how limited or open their own conception of gender was.

But before meeting any of them I first had to screen messages left on the voice mail. Let's get real—at the beginning I talked to almost everyone because I really wanted to get laid. And I wasn't as picky as I am now. I was an adolescent—it was time to experiment! Despite seeing hundreds of male clients while working as a professional dominatrix over a span of two years, my experience with men as partners up to that point had been somewhat limited: never having a boyfriend in my life, having had sex with three men (once with each) before I came out as a lesbian at nineteen. How would it be different now? And what kinds of men would be interested in me?

At that time I couldn't conceive that a gay man would want to be with me because of what is and isn't between my legs. Some of that was confirmed initially. I placed my ads in the "Men seeking Men," "Bi," "Trans," and "Other" sections, and I never got a response from "Men seeking Men." For the most part, female-to-male transsexuals are still unknown to mainstream culture. When most people hear or use the word "transsexual" it is understood to mean male-to-female. And there is certainly no pornography (that I've seen) about us. After being approached about being part of a slick "out-there" show on sex by one of the cable networks, and asked if I would possibly model nude, that show was dropped. I asked the researcher (who was quite hip and initially enthusiastic) to tell me the truth. She said that the two producers were a couple of straight guys who couldn't see how they could make an FTM transsexual be sexy. Sexy to them. While MTF transsexuals are fetishized in pornography (as part of someone else's fantasy, not their own) FTMs have been invisible. And so it follows that most guys answering my ads would be uninformed.

Bruce left only his name and number on my personals voice mail. I called him back.

"Your ad sounded tantalizing."

"Umm hmm...."

"So...how long ago did you begin your sex change?"

"I started hormones a year and a half ago."

"Hmmm...I don't mean to be disrespectful—but what does your body look like?"

"I have what *resembles* female anatomy, but otherwise I look like a man."

"But with your clothes off...?"

"Are you mostly interested in men, or women, or both?"

"I'm heterosexual," he says.

"Well, I doubt that you'd find me attractive, then."

"I'm attracted to masculine-looking women."

"I'm not a woman. People tell me I look like a gay man.... Have you been with transsexuals before?"

"Yeah, once. It was a really *interesting* experience. I'll never forget it."

"Male-to-female, or female-to-male?"

"Uhhh...male-to-female. I played with her cock.... What kinds of things do you like to do in bed?"

"It depends on who I'm with."

"Maybe we can get together...."

"Look—I did not place this ad to be an exotic experience for someone else. Besides, the kind of men I'm attracted to are mostly gay men or
gay-identified bisexuals—do you understand?"

"Yes. Maybe we can get together?"

"I don't think so. It wouldn't work."

Sometimes the sex has been great and I've had a lot of fun. The times
it hasn't clicked have mostly been with men who described themselves
as bisexual, but essentially led straight lives or had straight lifestyles. It
usually worked up to a point, and then they lost their erections. After
having a whole string of those, I asked one guy: "Is it the chemistry or
my body, or what?" thinking, because this was happening with such fre-
quency, that I must be a lousy lay. He said it was partly chemistry, but also
guys sometimes lose erections in new and unfamiliar situations. I guess
I'd qualify for that. Then he said to me: "You responded like a woman
when I was fucking you." And I wish I'd said to him: "Have you ever
fucked a man? Do you know how a man responds?"

I'm not typical of most transsexual men, in that I enjoy being fucked
in my vagina with a penis. The whole point of my gender transition was
to free myself up. If something feels good to me, I'm not going to stop
doing it because it doesn't fit someone else's notion of what a man is. And
as much as I can show bravado about the whole thing, sometimes I feel
very shy—that first of all, I was a boy born with a vagina, and second,
that I actually enjoy using it. Although I'd like my genitals to be different, for right now I can deal with what I have.

A guy named Carl left a message saying he'd like to talk.

"I'm looking for a new experience."

"Are you attracted to men?"

"No. I'm straight."

"You should know then, that even though I still have the plumbing I was born with, I'd look like any other guy to you."

"But you have female genitals, right?"

"Sort of…my clitoris has grown a lot. It's about two inches long when erect. It looks like a very small penis."

He wanted to come over and meet me anyway. As he walked in and sat down, he barely looked me in the eye.

"Aren't you supposed to like women?"

"My gender identity, which is who I feel I am inside, is a different issue than sexual orientation, which is who I'm attracted to."

He was already overloaded and this tipped him over the edge.

"You know, a lot of guys have a hard time with this. It brings up a lot— like thinking that if they're turned on to me, maybe they're gay."

His eyes flashed with recognition and he laughed nervously. As I showed him out through my narrow hallway, he walked past making sure that no part of him touched me.

It's a common expectation of men I meet through the ads that I look like a masculine woman or a butch dyke. I have explained again and again, ad nauseum, that I have sideburns, a goatee, a hairy belly—hair all over. That if they saw me on the street they would think I was like any other guy. Is that emphasis enough? But many are still surprised when they meet me. Another assumption is that now that I'm a "man" I should want to be with women and that I would automatically want to assume the "male-dominant" role in sex—in other words, acting out the traditional "hetero" dynamic.

I got a message from a crossdresser named Annabelle, who said:

"It sounds like we'd be perfect for each other."

"What are you interested in?"

"Everything."

"What specifically do you like?"

"Role-reversal."

"I can't imagine what that would be for me."

"Well, you know…I'm looking for someone to escort me. Someone to 'augment' my femininity."

"I don't think we're compatible."

Then I talked to Steve—or Sandra.

"Have you been with guys before?" I ask.

"No."

"Are you attracted to guys?"

"No."

"Then why did you call me?"

"I have this fantasy. Me dressed as Sandra going out with you. You're dressed as a man but really a woman."

"This is not about dressing up, for me."

"Oh, I understand."

"No. You really don't."

I really try to be forgiving because I know most people just don't have the information. I can't blame them for their ignorance—but sometimes I get so angry. I burn out from constantly having to explain myself. Fortunately some guys just innately "get it" and those are the ones with whom I end up having a great time.

I've always felt an inherent power imbalance in hetero relationships. It's unavoidable because of the culture's implicit (and explicit) expectations of gender roles and behavior. It feels quite alien to the way I'm wired. Which is probably why I have always been queer no matter what gender I am. Aside from all I have yet to understand about my own desire, I do know that a relationship starting out with an equal power balance has always been important to me. That can be a safe springboard into exploring erotic power-exchange in a more conscious way.

What I've learned through doing the Personals has been crucial in forming my new identity. By putting myself out there, I got to find out how I want to be related to and also what is unacceptable. That aside—I *love* sex and that's *really* why I do it! Most of the men I've met, and/or with whom I've had sex, have been very personable. Some guys, even though I am a totally new phenomenon to them, have treated me with great respect and made the adjustment very well. These are usually guys whose main interest is men. It's with them that I've had the hottest sex. I would guess this is because in being being conceived as gay out in the world, one is confronted by society's views of homosexuals as "less than men" and "like women." And this can lead to questioning one's own gender in a way that most heterosexual men never have to. So, having had to find a place in the world as a man on one's own terms, very often it is less of a leap on a visceral level for these men to experience me as just another type of man.

As much as others have had assumptions about me, I have also had to challenge my own preconceptions about men—particularly having been raised as female. I assumed that all gay men were "size queens" and that none would want to be with me because I have a pussy and a tiny dick. I'm discovering that there are plenty of fags out there to whom that's not important. For many, it's about masculinity in all its possible expressions, a dick being only one aspect of that. I also had this idea that a gay man (or any man for that matter) would automatically have a more positive body image and comfort with their sexuality than me, because they have the right "equipment." I was wrong. If anything, it's shown me that I'm not doing too badly at all, and that most people have something about their body they're not quite satisfied with and would like to change.

My sexuality has shifted enormously since my transition. At first when

I started having sex with people I met through the ads, old "programming" would creep in. I was raised to be a nice girl. I would have been called a slut if I were working the sex ads as a woman, the way I've been doing. But as a gay man, being told you're a slut is a compliment! There were times (early on) when I played with guys I wasn't really attracted to or didn't even like that much. After they'd leave I'd think, I can't believe I did that. It was partly horniness and partly not knowing my boundaries yet. Nowadays I am more confident that I'm desirable. Every transsexual I know wonders at some time—usually when they're in the first year or two of transition—if they are ever going to have a lover again, and if anyone is going to be attracted to them. I went through that—and sometimes I still do.

So how is sex different now? I actually feel like I'm in my body, which helps. I enjoy sex as recreation more than I did before and I'm able to distinguish between sex and romance whereas in my former incarnation, the lines frequently blurred. Definitely hormones. Since I began my second adolescence I've evolved into being a lot less dick-focused and more into the whole person—which is, after all, how I want to be related to.

Recently I have taken to posting ads online and have been (for the most part) getting better responses :

> Hi David: I'm a 39 yo Gay man living in SF. I'm 5'9",
> 190 lbs, bear-type. I have bright blue eyes and brown fur
> (including a full beard, which I wear short). I'm sexually
> adventurous, although more top than not, and male iden-
> tified (e.g., I don't care what's between your legs, as long as
> you are a man inside). I had many friends in the TS/TV
> community in Chicago, and have been looking for friends
> (as well as playmates) since I moved to SF 2 yrs ago. I'm
> HIV negative, and plan to stay that way. My interests

include music, both playing and listening, motorcycles,
photography, art in general, and roller coasters. I don't
smoke or drink. I have been told I have a healthy amount
of boy left in me.

Please drop me a line—I'd love to get to know you and
I look forward to hearing from you.

Greg

When I first started doing the Personals, I was telling a friend about it and reading her my ads. She asked:

"So, do you have gay sex with these guys?"

"What do you mean by gay sex?"

"You know, fucking in the ass."

So...if two women are fucking each other in the ass, are they having gay sex, or are they just fucking each other in the ass? What about when a woman is fucking a man in the ass? And what is it when a dyke and a fag have sex with each other? Or, when a man is fucking a man in the vagina? Is that heterosexual? As my friend James said to me after we had played for the first time: "Sex is not about body parts. It's about the erotic energy that happens between two people."

Lines in the Sand, Cries of Desire

Riki Anne Wilchins

For Joan Nestle

"We are the women who like to come, and come hard."
—Amber Hollibaugh

We spoke last week: just your average phone call. And then, just as we're getting off, you suggest I might want to write about the boundaries where my different selves meet: the complexity of this place, its borders and contours. And your suggestion leaves my face burning with shame and anger as if I had been struck: Who has ever wanted to hear such things, and where on earth is the boundary where a lesbian, a pre-operative transsexual with a cock, a woman, a femme, an addict, an incest survivor, and a post-operative transsexual with a cunt all intersect? Upon what map is it drawn, and upon what states does it border?

I have spent my life exploring the geography of this place, mastering unfamiliar terrain and alien customs, wandering regions as fresh, as uncharted, as inexplicable to me as private visions; surveyed its pathways as ignorant and blind as any first-time explorer, and finally discovered myself at day's end: lost, alone, bewildered and afraid. With time, my tracks have intersected and converged, crisscrossed again and again, until at last they have woven their own pattern: my life itself has become the place where these different selves meet, my skin the boundary which contains them, and the women in my life the states upon which it borders.

Now you say you want to hear about this place, its complexities and desires, its contours and terrain. It is one o'clock Saturday night, and at the moment I am more involved with the contours and terrain of the cock dangling about two inches in front of my face. I am forty-two, and I have been coming to this mostly straight, couples-only sex club in mid-Manhattan for almost a year now, working my way through acts successively more challenging and frightening for me, pushing back the boundaries of what I can do or imagine, practicing with newfound skill staying present and connected during sex, exorcising demons and ghosts by now so familiar I know their names and faces within an environment so anonymous I often don't know those of my partners. A place where straightforward sex is the commodity, physical beauty the currency, and lust the only coin. This is the ground I have chosen to confront my deep fear of butch or masculine sexuality, of possession and surrender, power and vulnerability, where I can finally recover the much, the many, the myriad ways and fragments of my life lost to incest, transsexuality, shame, and self-hate. I am trying to reclaim myself and I want my body back.

I want my body back.

I want my clit, my scrotum, my vagina, my cock, my beard. My buttocks, my thighs, my bush, my asshole, my urethra, my semen. My lips, my tongue, my wetness, and my saliva. I want my breasts back, the ones I watched go through a second complete puberty at twenty-nine. I want my nipples back, with the scars just beneath my pink aureolae where the implants went in, the left incision making the nipple over my heart mostly numb to touch or tongue. I want the scar on my throat, the one people notice, asking about thyroid conditions, the one opened to shave my Adam's apple down. And I want the scars you can't see, on the inside of my labia; the ones you get by doing the stitching from the inside, so they don't show. The ones which ache when I'm getting ill and itch strangely when I'm getting exhausted.

I want my body back.

I want the clear ejaculate which still trickles from my urethra when I come hard and fast. I want my clit back, the one the super surgeons, who can make almost anything into almost anything else, made by transplanting the very head, the glans, of my beautiful, long ivory pink and blue-veined penis right between my labia and then waiting three months for it to heal and the blood supply to stabilize; which, carved down in a second operation to the little clit-like apparatus I have now, is somehow still so sensitive it makes me tense and shiver as my sex partner's wife uses her left hand to open my lips and her right to rub it inquiringly, watching my face closely for any reaction and then smiling in satisfaction when my eyes unfocus, my stomach muscles harden, and my thighs spread a little of their own accord.

In my mouth goes his prick, tasting first of latex and then nonoxynol-9, which makes my lips and tongue go ugly bitter and numb. A little gag starting and then he is in my mouth and firming up nicely, the glans beginning to extend itself along my tongue and pushing up against the roof of my palate. An exciting and strange experience this, but stranger still is having had a cock and having had women go down on it, I'm unwillingly, suddenly, almost shockingly aware of how each movement of my lips and tongue must feel to him. Strange too, is that nerve endings which once made their home in my cock, and which now nestle in my cunt, are starting to remember too, and they're getting hot, turgid, and wet, and for several transcendent moments I cannot distinguish if I'm giving head to him, or to myself.

He is fully erect now, much like my dildo except the skin of his penis is very smooth and gripping it with both hands, I feel an unexpected softness around a firm core. After a moment I begin turning on my hands and knees, moving around on the mattress to face his wife as we begin to kiss. Her black hair is loose and shoulder-length, her mouth is soft and wet and opens to hard little biting edges which nip at my mouth, tongue and neck. I notice the small, downy hairs on her forearm glistening in the damp overhead light: its muscles work as she reaches for my cunt again, turning the hair blonde as it catches the light.

Exorcising demons and ghosts: I told my closest friend I was forty-one and knew nothing about men and didn't want to wake up at fifty-one and still know nothing, but the truth is much closer to the bone. The truth is that unable to outrun or contain the contradictions of my life, I had been celibate for the past five years. And with celibacy I had dead-ended into every cold and silent secret I had trailed behind me into a dozen monogamous relationships and scores of one-night stands but never once confronted, until at last it dawned on me, lying in a bed I had entered only hours ago and would never see again, my hand cradling my chin as I watched the sunlight slowly traversing the coverlet, that all my adult life I had successfully avoided anyone butch enough to turn me on or top me.

And so your question brings me back here, to things I dream of alone at night, to desires I acknowledge in the dark, to exposed edges and hot, melting shame. To the things about which I neither speak nor write, to the things about which I truly care and therefore make a career of avoiding. "Your writing is very direct," you said, "you're very in-your-face." Well I haven't had much choice. As far back as I can remember, my life has been a puzzle with missing pieces.

I hadn't even known the word "transsexual," nor that it was a word meant for me. In fact, I hadn't even known if transsexuals really existed, until at twenty-eight I read Christine Jorgensen's book and finally admitted to being one. A year later, strung out, a suicide note wound in the typewriter and the garden hose snaking from the exhaust pipe of my shit-green Volkswagen, I knew I would have surgery or have an end to it. I remember thinking I could always return to this place, but it would be a shame indeed if a livable life was waiting with a patient, indulgent smile on the other side of surgery and I had not lived to see it. So I hauled my weary white ass into the Cleveland Clinic Hospital's Gender Identity Program. But transsexual women were supposed to be straight, and I had never looked twice at a man, nor felt any erotic heat in their presence.

Determined to be a "successful" transsexual, I worked earnestly at being straight, at developing the proper attraction to men. I examined their firm little butts, learning to decipher which were cute and which not. I cruised the hair on their chests, their beards, their clothing and stance, the width of their shoulders and the bulge of their cocks, judging its length and thickness by the way it deformed the smooth, muscular profile of whichever jeans-clad thigh it was worn on. I faithfully reported each foray into heterosexuality to the hospital's noncommittal therapist, desperate to be the good patient upon whom she would confer surgery when my waiting time was up.

I finally informed her that I could not be straight, that I was, in fact, a compete bust with men, that the only thing which still gave me my somewhat limp, estrogen-impaired erections were other women. I knew then, suicidal as I was and living day-to-day only awaiting surgery, that when they threw me out I might make that trek out to the Volkswagen after all. "Oh yes," she said, as she peered up from my manila-foldered chart, "we had one of those last year," and she went back to writing case notes in my chart about my "illness," and I went back to breathing.

This was pretty amazing stuff at the time. The head of the only other gender program in town had solemnly informed me I could not be a lesbian. "All transsexual women," he declared, "want to be penetrated." Well, yes. But I thought maybe he knew even less about woman-to-woman sex than I did, and fearing his primitive sexual cosmology was accepted as revealed truth within the profession I hoped would save my life, I determined to keep my attraction to women as secret as my own pulse.

So I learned that I could be a transsexual, and attracted to women as well. But could I be a lesbian? Certainly the lesbianism into which I came out in the '70s said I could not. It told me then, as it often still does, that I was a surgically-altered male, a man invading "women's" space, my trespass tolerable to the precise extent I displayed the very oppressive, stereotypically feminine behaviors from which many lesbians were in headlong flight. As for what lesbians did in bed, the women's community into which I emerged reversed the statement of the doctors: "No lesbian," it solemnly intoned, "wants to be penetrated." Penetration, I learned, was for straight girls.

A transsexual she-male freak and a lesbian slut turned on by penetration in an orifice still under construction was bad enough, but even worse, I found out that the type of lesbian I wanted meant I was "into roles." I say I was "into roles," but in truth, it was all in my head. I learned from all quarters that "roles" were dead. Interred with them went the best of my desires: those strong, femmy butches who strode arrogantly across my dreams and scared me half to death with their power and my need.

And perhaps roles were dead, for in truth I saw neither femmes nor their butches at the few women's bars or functions I was allowed to attend. Even lesbians who professed support for "roles" were roundly ignored or actively reproached. The lesbianism into which I came out was dry and pale and bordered by bowl haircuts, no makeup, torn jeans, ubiquitous half-buttoned flannel shirts, and humorless, hurting women whose sexuality was firmly suppressed, politically obedient, and completely foreign to my own erotic tides.

I didn't know butches and femmes still existed, or even if they ought to, until you started telling me about them. You taught me the theory, and even more you taught me respect, resuscitating the femme parts of me with words like "complex," "courageous," "many-layered," and "specifically lesbian." "For many years now," you wrote me, "I have been trying to figure how to explain the special nature of butch-femme relationships to feminists and lesbian-feminists who consider butch-femme a reproduction of heterosexual models and therefore dismiss lesbian communities of the past and of the present that assert this style."

It was not until sometime later that you taught me the practice as well, and moreover that the women I craved still existed, that it was okay for me to want them and imagine them, to picture their hands and cocks and hunger as I lay across my bed, eyes closed and back arched, rubbing the middle finger of my right hand across my own recently-made clit and pushing the new dildo I'd trimmed to just the right size and shape deep into my own improbable, impossible cunt.

"Oh, my darling, this play is real," you wrote me once about your lover. "I do long to suck you, to take your courage into my mouth, both cunt, your flesh, and cock, your dream, deep into my mouth, and I do.... She moans, moves, tries to watch, and cannot as the image overpowers her...and then she reaches down and slips the cock into me.... I fall over her.... I am pounding the bed, her arms, anything I can reach. How dare you do this to me, how dare you push me beyond my daily voice, my daily body, my daily fears. I am changing; we are dancing. We have broken through."

And I wondered if I would ever break through, as I wandered through one-night stands and short-time lovers, remembered the details of their bodies but not their faces, their technique but not their words. I actively avoided the type of woman who turned me on, turned aside their gaze, saw them in bars and left. Each time some hidden place inside me burned with a pain I forbid myself to touch or explore, desires and needs which are well-described by words like "many-layered" and "complex," but which are far more distressing and aching than the crisp, black letters on the flat white pages containing them.

The truth is I had used sex but could not submit to it, and the truth is I could come but I could not be present in my body nor use it to express vulnerability or surrender. Sex was something I exchanged for safety or shelter or companionship. Sex was something to attract a lover who wasn't sure if she wanted a transsexual, and later sex was something to bind her to me through the shit she would take from friends. And after it was over, sex was a way to be a child again for an hour, maybe two, in safe warm arms.

Sex was a way to humiliate myself and my lovers, to suppress and yet simultaneously revisit again and again those childhood nights when the humiliation was mine and mine alone and the hot breath on my neck and back belonged to a complete stranger who only looked like my father and whom I met only in the dark. For the truth is, every time I tried to make love, the image of my father hovered above whatever bed I was in like some kind of demented crucifix hung on the wall over our heads, and the path I had trodden so long back to my sexuality, my body, and my lesbian self led in a beeline as long and straight and narrow as the lane-line down a flat-back Kansas highway right through to my father.

Incest is a word too ugly and short to do justice to something which is much more than simply ugly and too often not blessedly short. Incest is a daily thing, like the news, like dinner, like brushing your teeth. You can carry it around like a stick of gum in your pocket. It marks your body like a cancerous mole or a burn from hot cooking oil. It colors your thoughts like a drop of ink in a glass of water, and it poisons your life like shit down a well.

There are flavors and varieties of incest. There is the nice, simple kind that comes accompanied by clear, sharp snapshot memories developed by Polaroid. These are the ones you can take out and show your friends, who will commiserate; your therapist, who will analyze; and your family, who will deny. They are terrifying, but at least they have defined shapes, colors and dimensions, and also at least they are known.

Then there are those as hard to grasp as smoke, the invasions and violations not captured on neat Kodachrome squares, lacking specific memories and penetrations. This is the kind I remember best: just the sight and sense of probing fingers or too intimate caresses or special glances and the adult passions of a parent too hot and close and hungry for a needy child to understand. The kind which later in life announces itself with only vague and confusing physical and emotional memories, welling up without warning or reason from unknown and uncharted underground springs from acts carried out at an age so tender there were no words to frame and recall them; or perhaps a little older still, when words were at the ready and nearby, but quickly buried so well and far away they have no known latitude or longitude now but still manage to wake you from the dark in that familiar sweet sweat with your perpetrator's smell all over them, and your inner child screaming with fear and rage like a wounded banshee in the close night air.

And there is another kind of incest, a kind no one even names. This is the transsexual kind and it is a symphony of abuse. It is the Bach and Beethoven, the Haydn and Mozart of incest. It is orchestrated and complex, with woodwinds and strings, brass notes, and deep, bass rhythms. It involves forcing female children to live as boys, withheld hormones and medical treatment, and quick, vicious punishment by those people you love and trust the most for the slightest omission or infraction in dress or behavior. Its terrors and confusions culminate in a second puberty in the full glare of midlife adulthood, followed by a gaudy, baroque crescendo of doctors and scalpels and stitches and blood which, however good the surgery, still leaves you feeling violated and broken inside somehow and never quite sane in your body again.

And I am thinking of this, of your words and my life, as I feel his hands on me from behind now, warm and dry, rubbing gently on my buttocks, moving in widening circles until they pause and then dip between my legs, finding and then caressing the pink skin whose origins and construction I still cannot imagine. A single finger pauses at my cunt, stroking just inside my vagina and then tunnels slowly inward, so slowly in fact that I cannot refrain from pushing back, surprising myself with a soft moan which sounds vaguely ridiculous, even to me. Even to me, who has walked the halls of this place many evenings, just listening to the sounds of women caught in the distress of their own lust, their overheated cries and whimpers clutching at my damp insides like a strong hand or running clean through my body like an icepick through warm butter.

His finger slides out of my pussy now and I feel the first taut nudge of his cock. Holding it in his right hand, he searches patiently for my open, wondering vagina. After a year of work, my own dance is about to begin. You have helped to bring me here. I wonder: what will you think reading this? Will you be able to see the lesbian in me, in my experience? Have I come through so many rejections to face another? And if you cannot read this, and read in it other lesbian lives and identities and appetites and passions, then who will? I have heard my own echo in your voice. Will you hear yours in mine?

Our lives become the enactment of those things we can think, the erotic acts and petty daily defiances of the fears which haunt the borders of what we will confess to desiring, what we can imagine ourselves wanting to do with our own bodies and those of our lovers. The borders are not drawn by us, but by our fears, lines drawn in the sands of our need by rape or shame or abuse, imaginary lines in shifting sands we dare not cross. And standing beyond those lines are the women who have gone before, who have stepped past and returned to tell us what lies beyond, and about the parts of our lives we have lost, whose words we can read but not yet write, whose stories, at once terrifying and exciting, we carry around for years, running them over and over in our minds like old movie reels until at last we recognize them as our own, coming back to us like prodigal children returned in the night or the echoes of our own voices, thrown back at us from a cry of desire uttered so long ago, and in such pain, we neither recall it nor recognize its origins as our own.

He finds my vagina and gripping my hips, he uses both of his wide hands to pull me back onto his cock. I feel my body parting to take him in, a familiar-strange feeling of pressure-pleasure as he enters me confidently, until at last he is in my flesh up to the hilt. I am struggling to take all of him now, and to stay connected as well: feeling him, testing myself, tightening obscure muscles somewhere far up inside my vagina. He pulls me back, the air forced from my lungs as if someone has struck lightly at my stomach, and just as I catch my breath he begins to move, accelerating now, the apex of his thrusts going off like some liquid explosion deep in the center of my pelvis. I am filled with a kind of wonder now, my body showing me things novel and unsuspected.

In slow motion I close my eyes and collapse into his wife's waiting arms. They know it is my first time, and she gently gathers me in, her hands cradling my face, pulling it down and in between her legs. I begin to lick her thighs, her groin, her clit, anything my hungry little mouth can reach, the sweet-smelling hair of her bush containing the sounds now coming from my throat. She laughs, a quick, easy sound, as I raise my hips to take more of her husband's cock inside me. Her plump, buttersmooth hips are tightly encircled, my arms gathering her whole cunt onto my mouth. I suck on it viciously, teething like an infant with bottle while another part of me concentrates on withstanding each delicious withdrawal and fresh, fierce entrance. I am in a kind of heaven, and for the first time in my life I am present in my body and unafraid and I am on wings.

"We are the women who like to come, and come hard," Amber Hollibaugh said. "I am a femme, not because I want a man, but because I want to feel a butch's weight on my back, and feel a butch moving inside my body." And nice as his maleness is, it is neither female nor what I want and I begin to play with my head a little, imagining he is a woman and his dick, a dildo strapped on with a soft butch's contradictory, perfectly masculine arrogance. Pleased and emboldened by the effect she is having, she uses her knees to lever my legs further apart. "Is it okay for you, honey?" she taunts, holding me like that for long seconds, pressing into me, pushing relentlessly forward and down, purposefully using her full weight so I need all my strength to support us both.

She leans far forward over the long muscles of my back, taking her time to pinch each of my nipples, and then pausing to wipe the small beads of sweat which have collected at my temples. "What's wrong, baby, is it too much for you?" she purrs, and pulling me backwards she enters me so deeply the O-ring of her strap is suddenly clear and cold on my butt. I catch a glimpse of her over my shoulder, wearing the smile she flashes like a hidden blade, her teeth gleaming in the dim light with pleasure as my face contorts with that far-away look as if I'd heard the whistle of a train, high-pitched and way off in the distance. Her free hand slips beneath me, trails along my belly, oblivious to my hips jerking sideways, avoiding her, knowing her intent. She searches diligently for my clit, finds it, and begins to worry it, rubbing patiently from side to side with practiced, entirely successful fingers.

I am completely still now, holding my breath to deny her the reward of further response. Until something deep inside me just snaps, bursts clean; and groaning with rage and lust my back arches, a proverbial cat in heat, and she, laughing out loud, answers. Strong, veined hands grip my hips, and she makes the first, killing thrust that begins her final motion, and I know now that she will come fucking me, shouting hoarsely and thrusting into me just as hard as she is able. The warm honey-butter-blood begins to flood the cradle of my cunt and I realize that for once, my father is nowhere to be seen, no, nor my fear of masculinity and submission, of penetration and vulnerability, and closing my eyes to surrender to the first delicious tugs of orgasm, I know for the first time and with a certainty beyond simple trust that I am free.

A REAL GIRL
MICHAEL THOMAS FORD

"Suck my cock," he orders as I kneel between his legs and slip him between my lips.

He puts his hands on my head. I work on his dick. "I want you to think about how that cock is going to feel slamming into your wet pussy."

I take all of him into me, thinking very much about how his cock would feel slamming into my wet pussy, and my dick gets hard.

I was born into a house of women. My father was frequently away and even when he was home, he was generally eclipsed by the personalities of my mother and my sisters, who were already ten and eleven at the time of my birth and who seemed to fill the house to overflowing with their loud voices and their shining, laughing presence until there was no room left for the rest of us. Although my father and I enjoy a happy relationship now (both my sisters and my mother have left the house), when I think back on my childhood I cannot recall a single incident in which he was actually involved.

Nor can I with any real clarity recall my mother in those years, although she was certainly a much larger and much more constant figure in my life. I don't think she ever particularly liked men or wanted a son, and I know for certain that she had no idea what to do with the one she got. After having lost one boy child at birth, I suspect my appearance almost a decade later was more by chance than through careful planning, and she simply did the best she could under the circumstances. Since my birthday falls exactly nine months to the day from New Year's Eve, I imagine I have a bottle of champagne, or perhaps several, to thank for my presence in the world.

Being, as she most certainly was, from an era when mothers had daughters and fathers had sons, my mother probably assumed I was my father's
responsibility, at least so far as social conditioning was concerned. When it
became apparent that this just wasn't going to happen, she made the most
practical choice—she would raise me as she had her other two children.
Never mind that they were female. As a result, I grew up fairly oblivious
to the fact that other people felt there were differences between the sexes.
It helped, no doubt, that most of my friends were also being raised by their
mothers and sisters while their fathers, who like mine were employed by
the government, worked long hours doing whatever it was men did in
those days when the Cold War rumbled on and governments spent a great
deal of time trying to figure out what the others were up to.

In the end, I grew up thinking that there was very little difference
between my sisters and myself. When they began to notice boys and date
them, I found nothing odd in the fact that I, too, was attracted in some
way I didn't entirely understand to the young men who came to the
house. I recall vividly one of my oldest sister's boyfriends, who would
drive up to the house in his big, grumbling TransAm with the ubiquitous
firebird painted across the hood. Unshaven, sporting a white T-shirt and
worn jeans, he would lean against the car and smoke while they talked.
Lying on my bed in the room above them, I would listen to their conversations through the window and think about the time he had scooped
me up in his big arms and swung me around until I was dizzy from the
motion and the smell of his aftershave.

"So, you like it rough?" he asks. "You want me to fuck you hard?"
*I look up into his dark eyes, which stare down at me unblinking, waiting
for me to ask him for what I want. "Yes," I whisper, and my breath leaves me
as his cock enters fiercely.*

Years later, I would begin to have sex with men myself. And the men
I found myself attracted to the most were the kinds of men my sisters and

their friends had dated. Big, powerful men, filled with a masculine spirit that surrounded them like the tight T-shirts they invariably wore. Nothing like the superbutch gay clones of the 1970s, nor the gym-made bodies of the '80s and '90s, the men I desired had developed their ways of moving and talking from years of walking through the world as men, taking up more than their share of space and firmly believing that much was owed them simply because of their sex.

Unfortunately for me, these men were almost universally straight. This didn't, of course, prevent me from becoming fixated on them, nor did it always stop them from having sex with me. But very, very seldom did I find the passion and intensity I was looking for, the powerful desire I had always imagined making love with a man would involve.

The problem, I realized after several years of disappointing sex, is that I wanted a man to make love to me the way that a straight man who really loves women would make love to a woman he wanted more than anything else in the world. I have no illusions about the failings of heterosexual attraction, and certainly I have never idealized the male-female coupling as better than any other. But there is, I think, an intensity of need that accompanies the way a man who truly desires a woman will approach their lovemaking that I think is missing from the way most gay men make love to other men.

Partly, of course, this is due to the sex roles we are taught from childhood. Whether we admit it or not, most of us are preconditioned to one degree or another to respond in certain ways during sex. Men pursue. Women are pursued. While gay men have managed to escape many of the constraints of traditional male roles, we are still fundamentally male, and I think many of us still find it difficult to respond to one another sexually in ways that we are taught are inherently female. This has nothing whatsoever to do with issues of passivity and dominance, of top or bottom. Those are categories of action that make detailing the actual physical activities we engage in easier. Someone is fucked; someone does the fucking. One partner is whipped, the other is the whipper. Neither role is fundamentally male or female, although many times we try to assign these values to them in order to make sense out of them.

No, this is about allowing or restraining the expression of need and wanting. It is about an ability or a willingness to be seen as an object of desire and respond accordingly, to weigh and measure a partner's needs and either meet them or use them to heighten sexual play. Gay men, as men, are perhaps more afraid even than their heterosexual brothers to admit needing something from a partner, or to admit to wanting to be desired, and often this results in sex that, while providing a release, frequently fails to transcend simple fucking.

"Don't talk," he says while I tell him how my dick feels in his ass. "I can't come that way. Just fuck me."

It's curious to me that gay male culture, which as a whole has provided enormous opportunities for men to express themselves in most other areas of life, is perversely limiting when it comes to sexual play. While we may feel free to engage in sex more frequently, openly, and gymnastically, thereby creating a glorious illusion of increased freedom of expression, we continue to rigidly define our sexualities with categories like top and bottom, butch and femme, master and slave. Perhaps we will admit proudly to being "versatile," as though we are some kind of unique sexual accessory for all seasons, but in general we have a limited sexual repertoire, a handy list of activities that will result in an orgasm. Even the world of S/M, which certainly provides some of the most positive opportunities for exploration and fantasy, involves a structure which relies heavily on its participants acting according to strict rules.

"I went to the baths and had sex with seven different men," a friend tells me.

"What was it like?" I ask.

"What do you mean?" he asks, puzzled. "We fucked. We came. It was really hot."

"But why was it so hot?"

"I don't know. It just was."

See, this is the problem. In our mad scramble to get away from the puritanical sexual ideals most of us were raised with, we've defined sexual expression in quantitative terms. The biggest cocks. The hardest bodies. The most orgasms in a single night. All fine and good, certainly. But somewhere along the line, we've forgotten how to explore. We've forgotten why we want those hard cocks and those body-shaking orgasms.

The best sex I've ever had occurred after months of foreplay. I met the man and was instantly attracted, but his lover stood in the way of anything happening between us. Still, every Sunday afternoon he would show up at my house, ostensibly just to talk. We wanted each other badly, yet neither made a move. Inevitably, we sat next to one another on the couch, flirting in our own ways but never doing anything about it, until finally he would leave and I would masturbate furiously, unloading my need onto my stomach while I imagined him kissing me.

Then one afternoon—I don't remember why—he began to tickle me. The next thing I knew, I was over his knee, and he was rubbing my ass through my shorts, telling me how bad I was for getting him all horny. I almost came just from the unexpected pleasure of his finally touching me in a sexual way. Nothing more happened that day. He was too anxious about his lover. But he came again the next Sunday, and that time he tied my hands behind my back with his belt and grabbed my cock through my shorts before leaving.

Each week we progressed a little further. One week he removed my shorts and fisted my dick while I begged for more. The next he allowed me to mouth his hardened cock through his pants. But nothing more. Neither of us ever came. I wanted him more than I'd ever wanted anything in my life.

One night he called me. His lover was out of town, and he wanted to know if I'd like to come over. I did. For several hours we sat on the couch, watching TV and desperately avoiding what we both wanted to happen. I think I spent the entire time hard, waiting for the moment when I could go home and bring myself off.

"I have to go," I said finally. "It's late."

"Not this time," he said, rolling on top of me and pinning me to the couch. His tongue went into my mouth, his hand went up my shirt, and after months of waiting, it began. I slept that night with his cum stained on my skin, thinking about how, just before he came, he said, "I've wanted you like this since the first time I saw you."

"Please," he says, "let me see it. Please, I'm begging."

I'm talking to my friend Shar about this subject, trying to sort out my thoughts. Shar, the queen of all femmes, sums it up easily. "Oh, honey," she says knowingly, "you want to be the object of desire."

She's right, of course. Women understand this. They understand the inherent power in being wanted for what they can give in a way that men don't and never can. Perhaps this is why so many of them are attracted to men who want them enough to do anything for them, men who, to outsiders, appear to have nothing to offer. It's why so many supermodels are married to ugly rock stars.

And I've found a way to get what I want. I've discovered the world of cybersex. Ever since getting my online provider, I've spent time visiting the numerous online sex rooms. It is in these areas—free from the normal pressures—that I find men can relax and explore their fantasies. Because it is all fantasy. You don't know who is on the other end of the conversation, typing the nasty thoughts that flash across the screen in neat little boxes. The online profiles users can create are, I suspect, about as real as the bios for Hollywood celebrities. In fact, a casual glance through several dozen shows that the typical male user is six two, a hundred and eighty pounds, exceedingly handsome, with an eight-and-a-half-inch cock. Given the law of averages, I find this hard to believe.

It doesn't really matter to me, however. What matters is what I can do with what I'm given, and on a good day that can be substantial. I have had endlessly fascinating encounters with a wide variety of men, from those who are looking for a first time with another man to those who describe in glorious (and frequently horribly spelled) detail exactly what they wish for me to do to them, or them to me. I am helped, I suppose, by the fact that I've written pornography for many years. My online persona is, in fact, one of my male pseudonyms brought to cyberlife. Sometimes I am struck by the fact that I, too, have turned myself into fantasy in order to do these things, but my profile is accurate, even if the name has been changed.

But still there are disappointments. "What do you like?" a prospective partner asks.

"I like making a man come because I've fulfilled one of his fantasies," I respond.

"But what do you like?" he asks again. "Do you fuck or get fucked? Suck or get sucked?"

Gay men like lists. They like options that they can tick off once they've been explored, like assignments waiting to be finished. Sucking dick. Getting sucked. Fucking. Getting fucked. Sexual play is defined by what you like, not by what you enjoy feeling.

"It depends on the man," I answer. And on the situation, too. But it would take too long to explain that sometimes I see a man on the subway, and the way he's holding his newspaper makes me wish that he would push me up against a wall and shove his dick up my ass. And other times I see a man carrying a package, and the way his sleeves are rolled up his arms makes me want to fuck him until he comes all over himself. I "like" many things, but most of all I like what leads up to them and fuels the encounter.

I suppose it was only natural that I would eventually turn my attentions in another direction and create a female persona for my online wanderings. Thus was Lily born. No sooner had I written her profile (personal quote: "If you want to see it—beg") and signed on than I was besieged by men demanding my attentions. Some, of course, were of the "want to suck my cock?" variety, and were quickly squelched. Others, however, were seriously interested in courting Lily, and wooed her steadily until they got into her head and, at least on screen, into her bed.

I discovered quickly that, like me, Lily has a penchant for rough, demanding men. And like myself, she has many moods. Some nights she likes to be made love to slow and easy while a man pleasures her to climax with his hands and mouth. Other times she likes it fast and nasty, bent over a crate in an alley as someone shoves his cock into her pussy and bites her neck while another pushes his dick into her mouth and comes down her throat. Still other times she plays the stern dominatrix, dictating every step in the fantasy. For several months she met regularly with a New York City policeman who loved nothing more than when she ordered him to fuck himself with a flashlight while she called him names and he begged to lick her pussy clean.

Mostly, Lily likes it when she gets men to open up and tell her what they really want. She doesn't care what it is; she just wants to hear them say it. She longs for the moment when they give in and type the words, "Please, I want to feel your pussy around my cock. I want to fuck you."

Better yet are the times when she breaks through and discovers a man's secret fantasies. "Do you want me to fuck you in the ass?" she asks.

"I don't do that," comes the reply, and the challenge is on. Lily knows all men like it in the ass. She teases. She coaxes. She slips a single finger into his hole while sucking his cock and seduces him with her nasty mouth.

"Please," he types suddenly. "Please fuck me now."

Pleased, Lily complies.

"Are you a real girl?"

Am I a real girl? The first time I encountered this question, it was posed by a married man who was jerking off at his computer while his wife slept in the next room. She wouldn't suck his dick, he said, and he desperately wanted to lose his load in a woman's mouth and have her swallow his cum. Lily was happy to oblige, but first she wanted to know about his dick. "What does it look like?" she asked. "Describe it."

The man was suspicious. No woman, he said, had ever asked him what his cock looked like. They didn't care. I did. I wanted a visual, however concocted, of what I was supposed to be sucking. He didn't know how to respond. "It looks like a cock," he said finally.

Another difference, and an important one. As a gay man, I am used to assessing men based on their cock size. "How was he?" a friend will ask about a recent encounter.

"Great," I say. "Big dick."

But really what I mean is, "I loved the way the skin below his balls tasted when I licked his asshole and he moaned because no one had ever done that. And I loved the way he pressed his cock against my belly when he kissed me, as though he couldn't wait to get inside me, and how he sucked me through my boxer shorts." But what I say is, "He had a big dick." It's our shorthand, and it (sort of) works.

As Lily, I've slowly learned to let go of those ways of measuring the success of an encounter. Whereas in person I may be conscious of my less-than-perfect abs, or wonder whether or not my partner's asshole has been recently washed, in cyberspace I don't care. "Suck your pussy juice off my dick," someone will say, and I do, not thinking about how big it is. "Stick your fingers in my ass," I tell a man who is eating me out, and when he does I love it.

Yes, this is fantasy. It isn't real. Yet in many ways it is more real to me than actual sex. It's real because we are telling each other what we want. In order to type the words, we have to think about them and put our desires into concrete form. A simple "fuck me" does little to elicit a response, whereas "I want you to stick your dick in me slowly—fuck just the opening of my cunt until I ask for more" is an admission of desire. "Suck my cock" is nowhere near as effective as "Work your lips over the head and lick it slowly, tasting the precum. See how horny you've made me."

And yes, the sex is better as a woman than as a man. As Lily, I feel desired. There is something about a man begging Lily to let him fuck her, or asking her to whip him, that arouses me much more than any man asking me, as a man, to suck his cock or fuck him. Perhaps it's a stereotype, the woman being pursued by the man. The princess and the knight in shining armor. The romance novel heroine, bodice near to bursting, being deflowered by the randy stablehand. So be it. It makes me come.

I do not want to be a woman. I love inhabiting a male body. I like the way it moves and smells and responds. I love having a dick and feeling it hard in my hand, or feeling it slide into a warm mouth or asshole. I love the feeling of a cock pushing its way into my ass. I love coming, and the way my load splashes over my belly and sticks to the hair of my forearms. I especially love the way my body feels when it touches another man's, both familiar and alien at the same time.

No, this is not about wanting to be a woman. It's about wanting to be free from the boundaries created by expectations, roles, and fears, and even from the limitations of my own genitals. It's about wanting to desire someone or be desired in turn, without worrying that something isn't exactly right. I like it when a man begs to put his mouth on my pussy. I love it when he tells me he wants me to bend over so he can fuck me from behind. I come with him when he can't hold back any longer because of what I say to him and he loses his load all over my tits.

Yes, I am a real girl. And yes, I am a real man.

TECTONIC SHIFTS:
CROSSING CULTURES,
MAPPING DESIRES

Criticizing our own culture's hidebound ways is one thing, but it's truly eye-opening to peek over the "wall" and see how things change under the influence of different cultural assumptions and identities. We offer here only a tiny taste of the rich identity soup that simmers globally, but it's enough to point out to us that the United States aren't the whole world; internationalists are reminded all the time that most aspects of our cultures are relative and mutable. Anthropologists, sexologists, and students of sex in history all help us document how differently sexual behavior and sexual and gender identity can be coded in different places, at different times, and within subcultures. Without such a transhistorical and crosscultural perspective, we fail to see not only the diversity that exists and has existed, but also the diversity that may yet exist thanks to the inexorable process of cultural change.

It seems obvious that contemporary American sexual identity politics play a role in transforming U.S. (and, to a degree, Western) culture, fitting into a larger pattern along with changes wrought by the Pill and penicillin, advances in abortion technology, the advent and gradual control of AIDS, and the sexual and feminist revolutions. But into what are we transforming? The emergence of "pomosexuals"—people who don't quite fit the pattern of these emerging sexual identities—may point the way towards a still-diversifying future.

Lawrence Schimel examines the parallels between gayness and (American) Jewishness, and the cultural changes happening within both identities. David Tuller's visit to Russia's emerging queer community turned some of his entrenched notions about sexuality upside down. As a result he not only looked twice at formerly unexamined American biases; he let Russian ideas affect his own self-image and sense of the possible.

DIASPORA, SWEET DIASPORA:
QUEER CULTURE PARALLELS TO
POST-ZIONIST JEWISH IDENTITY

LAWRENCE SCHIMEL

The other day, my sister remarked that I was looking "less gay." What she meant was that I looked more masculine—thereby exposing her own (well, society's) prejudices about effeminacy and the often-widespread notion of gays being "less than men." I have, in fact, never looked more gay: I have a close-cropped buzz cut, a goatee, and the results of a year's worth of working out in a gym. In fact, the only thing I'm missing to be a perfect '90s clone is a tattoo, something tribal perhaps, on my left or right arm.

But I'm a Jew, and Jews don't do tattoos.

While I don't practice Judaism, I was raised a Jew, and that cultural heritage is hard to shuck off. A tattoo would preclude my being buried in a Jewish cemetery, and while this issue of where I'll be buried is something that I hope will remain a long way in the future, being buried with my family in the Jewish cemetery where I already have a plot is something that I'm not sure I want to give up. I may change my mind someday, renouncing the restrictions of the cultural identity I was born into (Jew) in favor of one I have chosen (fag), but until then I'm heeding, or at least not challenging, Jewish custom and law.

My being a Jew is more or less an inescapable, irrefutable fact because I was born to a Jewish mother, the most-widely accepted criteria for Jewish identity. Even were I to convert my religion, many people—Jews and non-Jews alike—would still consider me to be racially or ethnically a Jew.

Because my being gay was not apparent or known—to myself or anyone else—until later in life, my homosexuality is seen to fall in a spectrum of identities, because there was a time when I (like all children) was heterosexual-by-default. Queers are born assimilated, we're raised to be heterosexuals, and only later in life do we separate ourselves from straights— not so much to defy their homophobia as to help us find each other.

Being gay was for a long time thought or said to be "just a phase"— odious and pejorative rhetoric, to be sure, but one which I prefer to the notion of genetic causality now in vogue. My discomfort with this new position stems from its inherent presupposition that, if one had a choice, one would obviously not choose to be gay. Being "born gay," we're guiltless for our sexuality—which, admittedly, may have been a useful response to the repressive psychiatric notions that homosexuality could or should be "cured," but one which gets my dander up. Given my anxieties about disease, about passion and love, my decisions to have sex are quite conscious.

I may have been born a homosexual, with a biological inclination or preference toward sexual activity with members of my own gender (assuming, for the sake of this argument, a rigid bipolar gender system with no blurring or reassignment or other gray area), but I *choose* to be gay. I signify this physically by adopting the muscle-clone look so prevalent here in Chelsea, New York City, where I live, and in much of the gay media, even if I don't practice all the rituals (drinking, drugging, smoking, partying) of the clone lifestyle. I am not simply someone who happens to have sex with other men; I am choosing to live a gay lifestyle, in a gay ghetto, and writing largely (though not exclusively) on gay concerns. I have willfully adopted and constructed an identity based on my sexuality (easy enough to do as a post-Stonewall baby, given the freedoms, liberties, and rights won by queers who lived and fought since before I was born) and therefore resent this notion that I was born to be queer. (It's a good thing I'm not Protestant, since I'd have the same problem with predestiny vs. free will!)

The idea of being "born gay" presupposes a rigidly bipolar sexuality, Kinsey zero heterosexuals and Kinsey six lesbians and gay men, which I know, from my own experience and those of the people in my life, to be far from the case. Gay sex and sexuality transcend racial, religious, class, and other identities—we recognize a unique kinship across all these various divides. And in fact we often romanticize these differences, eroticizing, for instance, working class men as the most masculine and therefore "least gay."

A Jewish identity also supersedes class (and to an infinitesimal degree racial) difference, for a Jew is a Jew regardless of other aspects of his or her background. But when it comes to sex, we do not always look to other Jews—although it is assumed by our families that when it is time to settle down and raise our own family we will choose a Jewish partner. What is taboo or "other" often becomes eroticized through our fascination with it—as an American Jew, I am fascinated (if sometimes also unnerved) by the foreskin I lack. "*Shiksas* are for practice," goes a joke among Jewish men, using the pejorative Yiddish term for non-Jewish women, who are okay to fuck but not to marry.

My mother is happiest if I'm dating a Jewish man rather than a non-Jew, even if she'd prefer I found a woman to marry (and she'd settle for a *shiksa!*). She also fits to a T the cultural Jewish mother stereotype of wanting me to find a doctor or a lawyer, and there was a time when I stopped being the black sheep of the family by bringing home a nice Jewish boy with a profession—real estate—at a time when my sister was dating an Irish Catholic. While my upper-middle-class family would prefer that my sister marry a well-to-do Jewish man, they'd prefer a poor Jew over a wealthy Latino or African-American. There is another Jewish joke, "*Tsuris* is a Yiddish word that means your child is marrying a non-Jew." (*Tsuris* is Yiddish for "intense aggravation.")

What the Jewish community fears, of course, in these intermarriages and relationships, is assimilation. We define ourselves by our otherness, our separation and difference from the goyim, those who are non-Jews. In my experience, nowhere is our Jewish difference more apparent than in an interfaith relationship; my Jewish friends in mixed-faith relationships have a far stronger sense of their identities as Jews and an awareness of Jewish culture and tradition than the Jewish couples I know.

We hold onto our Jewish difference so as not to disappear, even while we may crave a kind of "invisibility" where our Jewishness is merely another aspect of our personalities—the way I am a writer or my mother a teacher. Jews would continue to be Jews even in the absence of anti-semitism, whereas I'm not sure that there would be a need to be gay if the homosexual act were ignored instead of vilified. The existence or possibility of a similar gay invisibility, in contrast, is a myth in our current culture, since being closeted or passing is not some mythical haven but a cessation of identity and existence. When I have sex with another man—regardless of his race, class, or religion—the very act of our congress is the fundament on which our gay difference and community is based upon. There is no gay equivalent to inter-faith assimilation, merely denial.

I have a very public gay persona, particularly since I've written about sex I've had with other men, and often write generally (such as now) about gay sex and sexuality. Many of my books are specifically intended for a gay audience (even if occasional others read them). This presupposes the existence of such an audience, and my being a part of this cultural group.

When I say I'm a gay man, what I mean (and what everyone automatically assumes) is that I like to have sex with men, primarily if not exclusively. That's all. Being gay is presupposed to be a performative identity—that is, my identity is based on or reinforced by this act of desire, if not the sexual acts themselves.

My identity as a bourgeois American Jew is much less performative. Ostensibly I am meant to go to temple and pray, to observe Jewish custom and laws. The fact that I do none of these things provides no hindrance to my self-identity as a Jew—I have a secular identity as a Jew, completely divorced from the practice of Judaism.

Is it possible for me have an identity as a gay man, similarly divorced from the homosexual acts that are the literal process of being gay? Certainly I consider myself gay even if I have not actually had sex with another man in whatever quantity of time one wishes to choose. There is no statute of limitations, or requalification criteria, that I must have sex with a man every set period of time or renounce my identity as a practicing homosexual (though as a young red-blooded American male, I try not to let it be too long between these identity-affirming episodes). Likewise, before I had sex with anyone, I recognized my desires for other men, even as I tried to deny their existence.

But what about me is gay, aside from these desires, whether they're acted on or ignored? I don't deny that I live my day-to-day life in a gay environment, but I am hard pressed to determine what is authentically gay about it.

West Coast thinking would have me believe there is a gay spirit or sensibility which infuses everything in my gay life. Is it because I'm a born New Yorker that I resist this thinking, or is it in much the same way that I bridle at the notion of genetic causality for my sexual identity?

We have a gay culture: art, literature, media by gays and about the gay experience.

We have created gay communities, our semi-mythical mini-Zions: San Francisco's Castro, New York City's Greenwich Village and Chelsea, Provincetown, Fire Island's Pines and Cherry Grove, West Hollywood, Key West, Amsterdam, sectors of Berlin and London. (There are lesbian Zions as well: Northhampton, Park Slope, Palm Springs, etc.) These are our cultural homelands, and our visits feel like a return home, even if we've never set foot there before.

I like living in a gay ghetto. I take reassurance from it. I like walking down the street and cruising and being cruised, even if I'm not interested in whoever's cruising me or if the boy I've got my eye on ignores me. There's something about that moment of shared recognition of sexuality which builds community. I feel erased sometimes when I travel and heterosexuals don't even recognize that I'm cruising them—I feel I don't even exist.

I can feel this same sense of recognition when I meet Jews, although it is usually less visually oriented. There is a shared history, cultural references, identity. Although I find it lacking in the energy that gay cruising has, that outpouring of affability and desire and interest.

While I feel a bond of recognition when I meet fellow Jews, I also feel a twinge of embarrassment when I see Orthodox Jews, whose lives and lifestyles are so radically different from my own bourgeois Jewish identity. Where I live in Chelsea, I come into contact with the Chassidim daily, since the half dozen photo shops on my block are all run exclusively by Orthodox Jews who live in Orthodox communities out in Brooklyn and Queens and arrive by the busload each morning and depart the same way each afternoon. Their extremism is so distant from my comfortable secular Jewish existence, I resent being lumped in with them by non-Jews.

I think the Orthodox embarrass me in much the same way that assimilationist queers get upset by the outlandish openly-sexual modes of dress of the drag queens and leather fags in the Pride Parades. While the drag queens and leather fags are equally distant from the normative gay lifestyle I lead, I am unperturbed by their display and spectacle—I am in fact actively in favor of their inclusion in queer events—largely because my political and politicized identity as a gay man is one of my choosing.

I am a Jew by accident of birth, however, and am not ashamed of this discomfort the Chassidim cause me. While I identify strongly as a Jew, I am a post-Zionist American Jew who has also distanced himself from the practice of Judaism, which these Orthodox Jews so strongly represent with their distinctive, hirsute visual appearances.

When I talk about Post-Zionism, I am primarily talking about a change in Israel-diaspora relationships, though the term also applies to a school of thought that challenges Zionist thinking and is sometimes used to designate changes within Israeli society. I am a diaspora Jew, meaning I am descended from the tribes that have scattered across the globe and have not made *aliyah*, have not returned to the homeland of Israel. I have no desire to make *aliyah*; I plan to stay right where I am.

I was taught to pray in our common Hebrew language, though I was not taught the language itself. I do not understand the words I am pray-

ing, and I strongly resent this ignorance, the fact that I have these bless-
ings and prayers hardwired into my memory with no idea what they
mean. This linguistic alienation is only one aspect of my disaffection with
Judaism, though it reinforces my Post-Zionist identity as a Jew disinter-
ested in Israel as the sole focus of my Jewishness.

As the political climate in Israel in relation to the Middle East changes
and evolves, especially with the ongoing Peace Process, it becomes harder for American Jewry in general to maintain Israel as the vicarious
anchor of Jewish identity—if, in fact, it ever was. Zionism's primary goals
were to create a Jewish territorial, demographic, and political presence,
accomplished with the founding of the State of Israel in 1948, and to
achieve recognition and acceptance of this State of Israel from its Arab
neighbors. One of the major tenets of Zionism is the Law of Return,
which stipulates that any Jew anywhere can immigrate to Israel and claim
immediate Israeli citizenship. Historically, this option has held little
appeal for American Jews; according to Hanoch Marmari writing in *The
Jerusalem Report* on February 8, 1996, only 98,000 American and
Canadian Jews (an average of 2,100 each year) have made *aliyah*—less
than 1% of the Jews immigrating to Israel from around the world.

As I was growing up, before the fall of the Iron Curtain, American
Jewry mobilized to help Soviet Jews flee religious persecution and claim
this safety offered by the Law of Return. (At my temple, we children
went door-to-door among our neighbors selling macaroons and choco-
lates to raise money for Soviet Jewry.) A representative survey of
American Jews conducted in 1990, the National Jewish Population
Survey, shows that one-third of American Jews report making a contri-
bution to these established institutions during the year prior to the survey, and American Jews continue to funnel money to Israel via these
organizations.

My general feeling is that these contributions happen to a lesser degree
lately, which may simply be my distance from my Sunday School years when
I was regularly attending temple and being exposed to this information.

Perhaps it is because my peers, immediately post-graduation, can't afford to contribute money anywhere no matter how deserving the cause. But I think it is primarily due to the fact that, as the State of Israel's 50th anniversary approaches, there is less apparent need for such contributions—politically and economically Israel has become more independent than during my childhood.

Zionist thinking has often assumed that this philanthropy toward Israel provided a backbone for Jewish identity among diaspora Jews. My feeling is that the reverse is true: those Jews for whom their sense of identity as a Jew is important to them, those Jews who received a Jewish education and take part in and feel part of a Jewish culture and community, feel an imperative to support the State of Israel and its mission to protect and provide refuge for threatened Jews. I think the rest of us need some sort of threat to remind us to contribute; we don't feel Jewish because we contribute, but because we feel Jewish (and identify with the perils of being Jewish in a non-Jewish world) we contribute.

This element of peril is a galvanizing force toward community, as witnessed with the AIDS pandemic and its effect on gay culture. Before HIV was properly identified, the disease was referred to as GRID (Gay Related Immuno Deficiency) because it was first discovered among gay men and was considered to be "only" a gay disease, beginning the seemingly-inextricable linkage of gay identity and AIDS. ACT UP, Queer Nation, and other activist groups of gay men and lesbians coalesced because of AIDS and challenged the homophobic heterosexual culture to pay attention to this disease, to fund research toward a cure, and to treat those living with and suffering from the disease with the compassion and humane treatment they deserved. These groups came to represent a queer identity to the media, and united lesbians and gay men, politically and socially, across our often-separatist homosocial circles. Queers put aside their difference to fight our common enemy (in much the same way the religious right will put aside their differences to fight their common enemy: us). In many ways activism and a shared sense of outrage and frustration became the building blocks of our gay communities, as we fought for our lives and the lives of our lovers and friends.

More than a decade into the crisis, identity as an openly queer individual presupposes a political support of funding for AIDS research, even if it no longer presupposes approval or support of AIDS-related activist groups such as ACT UP. For a long time, diaspora Jews in America have felt that their Jewishness needed to inform their political views toward Israel, and especially Israel-diaspora politics, but this, too, is changing. We live in an era where an Israeli Jew has killed a beloved Israeli Prime Minister, Yitzhak Rabin. How are we to feel now, besides outrage and frustration? Why does death seem necessary to effect change, be it political or social? It took the Holocaust to cause the founding of a Jewish nation-state, thereby introducing Jewish concerns to the Western-centric stage of world history, and it has taken the ongoing devastation wreaked by AIDS to put queer visibility on the map of world events and politics. The cost, in both cases, has been too dear.

The persecution of queers continues from the heterosexual culture's intolerance if not outright hatred of our very existence. So much of our gay community and identity is formed in a reaction against this oppression rather than stemming from an integral authentic need or experience. I resent that the heterosexual culture manipulates our actions so strongly in this way, from our Pride Parades defying their homophobia-shame to our need for full-time watchdog organizations like Lambda Legal Defense and GLAAD, the Gay and Lesbian Alliance Against Defamation (paralleling the Jewish Anti-Defamation League).

In today's culture, a gay identity is perforce a necessary stage toward true sexual liberation, the freedom from all identity politics, the freedom not to need to define and justify our sexualities and sexual choices.

The Israel-diaspora relationships that comprised Zionist thought were likewise a necessary stage of religious liberation and protection for Jews; even within Zionist rhetoric, however, this was only a stage. An important part of the foundation of the Jewish nation-state is its independence from other countries (insofar as any country can be independent in today's global political community). Zionism-as-philanthropy is but one aspect of Jewish identity for American Jews, and it is largely dependent on the preexistence of a strong Jewish identity.

We post-Zionist Jews have begun to separate what is Zionist from what is universally Jewish, and one of the major Zionist tenets being overthrown is *shelilat hagolah*, the negation of the diaspora, the idea that all Jews will either make *aliyah* or cease to identify as Jews. In today's complex political climate, an assumed allegiance to Israel is no longer such a strong part of our Jewish identities; while still remaining globally-aware, we American Jews construct our Jewish identities closer to home and embrace our diaspora identity.

Gays are beginning to embrace our diaspora as well, choosing to stay home and come out wherever we are rather than moving to our mini-Zions of gay culture. And many of us in these Zions are choosing to leave, to form smaller enclaves outside of these arenas, to live queer lives in suburbia or rural sectors. We are learning to embrace our other cultural identities and still feel gay. The major factor driving most gays to our gay Zions is isolation and the need for community, but now it is possible not to be the only openly-gay man in Small Town, USA, and it is more and more possible to interact with gay culture through mass media—magazines, films, the internet—from anywhere in the world. Sure, it's fun to visit these cities, but they're no longer as essential to being gay as they once were.

Non-urban gay life seems inconceivable to so many of us, but I feel that way as a Jew, too. (I am, after all, a Jewish intellectual living in New York, so tradition and history suggests that I should stick around.) But for this Post-Zionist Jew and pomosexual, nothing is written in stone any longer, not the Ten Commandments of my Jewish forefathers nor the gay myth of Stonewall as the primogenitor of gay liberation.

Even remaining in one of the mini-Zions of both gay and Jewish life, the spectrum of my identity and opinions is constantly changing and evolving. By the time this essay is published, I may have shifted my position on either (or both) my gay or Jewish identities. Who knows, ten years from now, I may be leading a suburban Republican lifestyle, with a wife, 2.4 kids, a dog, a mortgage, and a picket fence.

Chances are likelier, though, that I'll have a tattoo, something tribal perhaps, on my left or right arm.

Adventures of a Dacha Sex Spy

David Tuller

The word *dacha* has no real counterpart in the English language. "Country house" comes closest, but that phrase's evocation of privileged comfort and exclusivity is far removed from the dacha reality that most Russians experience. Some dachas are grand affairs, three-story homes or large compounds reserved for prominent government officials and the newly rich; but for millions of city dwellers throughout Russia, the family dacha has always embodied associations far more profound than the attributes of the physical structure itself.

A dacha can be a shabby one-room shack, with a roof that leaks and no heat or running water. In the extravagant world of the Russian psyche, however, it is the essential locus of refuge and privacy; of warmth and nurturing friendships in the bleakest of times; of vodka-drenched toasts and tipsy flirtations that might or might not lead to passion or bed.

The first order of business upon arrival was to select a pair of *tapochki* (slippers) from the dozen or so scattered in messy stacks about the foyer. I quickly came to appreciate that custom observed in virtually every home I visited; the switch from street shoes to slippers served as a concrete symbol of the welcome transition from the harsh anonymity of public life to the warmth of Russian's remarkable hospitality.

Ksyusha, who at thirty-two was a couple of years younger than me, quickly became my best friend in Moscow and brought me to the dacha of Sveta and Lena, which possessed the magical charm of a folk tale. It had four cozy rooms: a kitchen off the foyer; a central chamber with two beds, a green couch, and various wardrobes and trunks; a den-like space with a dining table and a television set; and a tiny alcove with another bed and a solid wooden desk. It was not a large place, but it glowed with the intimate care that the occupants so scrupulously lavished on every detail.

We didn't do much, really, in the dacha, besides eat, drink, watch videos, and hold forth until the darkest hours of the evening; but it was always snug and entertaining and a good way to practice my Russian. Occasionally we took a walk through the woods of white birch or to the nearby pond; other times we just cocooned ourselves in the house all day and night.

The quiet way Ksyusha leaned her head on my shoulder when we danced at the dacha disconcerted me. She loved women, no doubt of that, but when she was younger she had been engaged to a boy she deeply loved, and occasionally she still slept with men—of whatever sexual orientation—she found attractive.

I explained that in the gay world where I lived, such behavior would outrage many lesbians, who would consider it a betrayal of sorts; that, in fact, the decision by many organizations to add the word "bisexual" to their names was causing an uproar and sparking anguished debates about the nature of sexual identity and the labels we used to describe it. Ksyusha shook her head in stunned dismay and emitted a torrent of commentary on the subject.

"That's just totalitarianism, just like the Communists," she snapped. "What business is it of anyone else's who I sleep with? You Americans, you feel like you need to define yourselves always, you are this or you are that. Why? You need to make up rules to follow, you all want to join in groups, to feel like you're part of something.

"But that's such a limitation, because then you don't act how you feel, but how you think you're *supposed* to act. So if I want to sleep with a man—please, thank you, did we have a good time? Yes? Wonderful, good-bye! What's the problem? Why should that bother anyone?"

Whenever my dacha friends would mention in passing that some Russian singer or actor was known to be gay, I would ask if the person was "out." This question always elicited a cascade of exasperated laughter.

"David, nobody is out here," they would explain with strained patience, as if admonishing a sweet but stupid puppy.

They thought it strange, too, that in this time of social and economic crisis of the early 1990s I had come to Russia to study gays and lesbians. It astonished them to hear that I had actually applied for journalism grants to conduct research on the subject, that anyone would entertain the idea of giving me money for such a preposterous proposal.

But I wasn't the *only* one interested in the topic, I protested. I told them about a sociology graduate student from Columbia University whom I had met in Moscow. He had come to Russia the year before to study some arcane aspect of the country's economic situation, but decided halfway through to examine homosexuality instead. He developed a detailed questionnaire about sexual practices and distributed it to men on the beach in Sochi, the Black Sea resort where many gays took their vacations. Someone in Sochi informed the KGB of the graduate student's activities. They arrested him in his hotel room and questioned him for hours, trying to pressure him into gathering information on gays for them; he refused. The whole affair spawned newspaper exposés about the American *seksualny shpion*, or "sexual spy."

This tale beguiled my dacha friends, and when I started doing my own interviews that is precisely what they dubbed me—"the American sex spy." I liked the nickname and decided to keep it.

As I continued to visit the dacha, I quickly developed a crush on Vitya, a hulking thirty-nine-year-old with a double chin and brooding eyes that narrowed to slits when he drank or laughed. Often he seemed distant, but occasionally I caught a flicker of silent torment cross his face; then his reserve would drop back over him like a thick woolen blanket. I knew that he and these women were linked in some deeply intimate manner; but how, exactly, I could not fathom.

I broached the matter with Ksyusha. "What's Vitya's story? Is he gay?" She rolled her eyes. "Vitya is...Vitya."

One day Vitya pulled down a red velour photo album from the shelf to show me "the family pictures." As I flipped through the pages, he provided a detailed explication: Here was Grigory, their friend who had moved to Spain several years back; a much-younger Ksyusha and her then-fiancé, Sergei; that was Toby, the black-and-white French bulldog that had died the previous year; ah, and Sveta, twenty-five years ago, wasn't she beautiful?

I peered at the photo; she was striking, certainly, with her saucer-round face and playful pout. I glanced at Vitya. He stared at the portrait, entranced; his mouth melted into an oblique smile, memory danced in his eyes.

Vitya was obsessed with Ingmar Bergman. The second time I was there, we watched Liv Ullmann, young and lovely, in *Persona*, a story of mental illness and merged identities; the third time it was *Cries and Whispers,* about three sisters and their maid. I had watched that movie as an adolescent, and the often spiteful behavior of the characters had baffled me. This time around, Bergman's tone of anguish and quiet despair plucked a melancholy cord in me—and, apparently, in Vitya.

"I've had my own cries and whispers, my own secrets, for twenty years now," he confided enigmatically.

I was curious, of course, but didn't want to pry. Actually, I *did* want to pry, but I wasn't sure how to. I rehearsed opening lines ("Vitya, I didn't quite understand what you meant last night...") and monitored the situation for opportunities. One evening, before I had a chance to make my move, Vitya and Ksyusha beckoned me over to where they were sitting. They wanted, they said dramatically, to tell me "the whole story."

It was weirder than anything I had imagined, and went something like this: Vitya had been lonely as a child, wracked by feelings he never understood. Other boys bored him, and he preferred playing with girls. As a university student, he formed a close friendship with three young women. "They took me as their own, like a girlfriend," he recalled. "They didn't look on me like they did the other boys, with whom they had romances, who they saw as potential sex objects. They told me their secrets, asked me advice about their affairs. I adored that kind of contact with them. Of course, the boys who came around thought it was very strange and wondered what I was doing with these girls."

Vitya himself did not quite know the answer to that question. Then, at the age of twenty-four, he met Sveta in a class for editors. They began to chat, discovered some common literary interests, and a *roman* (romance) developed between them. After a few months, Sveta introduced him to Lena—and they had all been together ever since. Ksyusha had entered their lives a few years later through family connections; her grandmother was a close friend of Lena's mother.

"Ever since I was a little boy, I felt like I was a woman." Vitya spoke in the slurred murmur of someone on the tenuous border between lucidity and tipsy incoherence. "And as I got to know Sveta and Lena, it struck me like a lightning bolt—I am a lesbian inside. I am not attracted to straight women, only to lesbians...."

"And if I hadn't found these two, I don't know what my destiny would have been," he added darkly.

He paused; we sat in a boozy haze in a corner of the room, and the dim yellow light cast eerie shadows on his face. His confession unsettled me: this tall, sexy man...a lesbian transsexual? I had been vaguely aware that people like that existed. But I had never actually met one before, and I pitied him.

"I thought Lena would be jealous of my relationship with Sveta, but at first she wasn't," he continued. "I think it was because she assumed that since I was a man, it wouldn't be a serious relationship. But then Lena realized it would last, and there was a lot of tension between her and me for several years. Until one day the three of us made love together, in this house, and the tension just went away."

"They made love right here, in this house!" Ksyusha added.

"And when you're with them, you feel like a lesbian?" I asked Vitya.

"Yes, of course!" Ksyusha interjected energetically.

I looked over at Vitya. He nodded vigorously and gestured toward his nipples, twitching his tongue back and forth gleefully and rolling his eyes in mock sexual ecstasy. Then he pointed downward. "I feel it there, too, but not as much."

"I have also been with him and the others, too, and it works down there, of course," asserted Ksyusha delicately. "But…that's not so important to him, he makes love like a lesbian."

The irony did not elude me—in the middle of this horribly repressive country, I had stumbled upon an elaborate web of romantic liaisons. Both Vitya and Lena still maintained intimate relationships with Sveta, and a deep and abiding friendship with each other; the addition of Ksyusha to the group had increased the possible sexual permutations. The four of them had sustained this unusual family life, off and on, for more than fifteen years.

"That is why I like Bergman," said Vitya. "I think he, too, has those lesbian feelings. Did you notice that all his movies have some lesbian theme in them? I don't think he could do that, understand that, if it didn't mean something to him personally."

Later that evening, we played a cassette tape with an eclectic selection of dacha favorites: French ballads, Sade, Roberta Flack, the Eurythmics. As Ksyusha swayed to the music, Vitya encircled her from behind with his brawny arms. He kissed her neck, ran his hands up over her shoulders and then, lightly, across her breasts; she closed her eyes and leaned back into his gentle caress.

There was something innocent and oddly touching in that gesture; watching them, I realized how much they had learned to accept each other through their years together. My pity for Vitya wrestled with awe and a little jealousy at the obvious devotion they all shared. Somehow, the dacha concept of lesbianism—very different from what I knew back home—allowed Sveta and the others to overlook the hard-to-overlook detail that Vitya was, in fact, a man. They let him be the lesbian that he believed he was, and he loved them back as only a woman could.

I wanted to understand Vitya's situation better, and he agreed to sit for an interview. He was excited by the prospect of discussing in depth what he acknowledged was his rather unusual sexual orientation. He had coined a term for himself—"inverted male-to-female transsexual"—to distinguish his predicament from that of men who longed to be hetero-sexual women.

Vitya had been aware of the specific nature of his feelings for almost two decades. But given the ascetic prudishness of the Soviet system, he first heard the term "transsexual" relatively late—only seven or eight years before. Since then, he had devoured whatever sexological literature he could find and firmly believed that such proclivities stemmed from biological and congenital roots rather than childhood psychological trau-ma. In fact, he had recently read an interesting article that suggested a connection between transsexualism and a difficult birth. That made sense to Vitya, since his mother had given birth to him with great hardship; for the first few days the doctors even doubted that he would survive.

Though Vitya knew sex-change operations were available, he never seriously considered that option. "I would have liked to have had a dif-ferent body, one that would interest lesbians more and not frighten them off," he acknowledged. "But I don't want an operation. For one thing, it would be hard to make a woman out of me—an operation wouldn't change my long arms, my long legs. Something womanlike would appear, but I still wouldn't be a woman. And the second thing is my age. I'm almost forty and have already somehow adapted to my situation.

"Sometimes I do feel very strongly that I would like it to be different, but I have learned how to cope with that. And since I have an extensive lesbian circle, I can get what I need from time to time—not everything, but almost everything. It's not perfect, of course. A good analogy to my situation is a person with a physical handicap, like someone without hands. He can make some mechanical adjustments and sometimes might not even notice what's missing—but something is missing all the same."

I asked Vitya if he remembered the first time he saw Sveta.

"Yes, I remember perfectly." A sweet radiance illuminated his face. "It was in this course for editors, and my first impression was that she was a woman who spoke very loudly and socialized a lot with everybody. She yelled during class, and basically disrupted everything. So I had mixed feelings. On the one hand she irritated me; on the other I was interested and amused. For the first few months we talked a bit during the course, we discussed this and that, and then I felt I wanted to get to know her better."

"Did you realize she might be a lesbian?"

"No, I didn't think about that at all, even though I knew she lived with another woman. Even when I first went to visit her and Lena in their room, I still didn't think about that. I just saw before me two wonderful, intelligent women, who were interested in what I was interested in. That day we spent three hours just talking, mostly about literature. And I saw that we all had a lot in common in terms of education, cultural interest, attitude toward life, toward art. I was delighted with that and wanted to get to know them better.

"But I didn't realize about their relationship until I went to visit them at the dacha and stayed overnight. When I woke up in the morning and raised my head, I saw that they were sleeping in one bed, opposite me, and they were lying down together in such a way that I immediately whistled and said to myself, 'Ah, so that's the deal!' At that time my romance with Sveta was just beginning, and when I realized that I was having a romance with a lesbian it excited me. It thrilled me."

It was through that arousal that Vitya finally understood his own lesbian sensibility. His concurrent discovery of the glories of Marcel Proust confirmed his understanding of his orientation. It was one of his pet theories that Proust, too, was an inverted male-to-female transsexual.

"By the time I met Sveta, I had already had a couple of experiences sleeping with straight women," he said. "And I felt that something wasn't quite right with that. It wasn't quite what I needed. Because the woman expected me to play a role that was not natural for me. She saw in me a man, a tough man, which I didn't feel like inside. And so that was a problem for me. The first time I understood why was when I met Sveta. After a while I told her, 'Sveta, I don't want to make love like men normally do with women.' She asked me, 'What do you want?' And I said, 'I want to make love to a woman as if I were a woman.' And she laughed and said, 'That's not possible.'

"But then I fell insanely in love with the work of Proust, because it was only there that I encountered someone like myself," he continued. "It was impossible to find Russian translations of Proust, but at the dacha a friend from Paris gave us all the volumes in French. At that time I didn't know French well, but I knew enough to catch the general meaning of it, and particularly one section where Proust describes how the hero suffers because his girlfriend sleeps with another woman. He suffers this agony, to an incredible degree, both about her actual and imaginary relationships with women. And he understand that he can't be like them, that he can never give the woman he loves what another woman can give her."

"How did you feel when you read that?"

"I was stunned, completely stunned." Vitya hunched forward in his seat; his words tumbled over each other with the rush of revelation. "Why was I stunned? At first I didn't really understand. I just knew it was incredibly important for me, more important than anything else I had ever read. And after several days I realized that it was about me. Because I've had situations like that, when I saw two women, two lesbians, and I suffered terribly watching them. It was clear to me that it wasn't jealousy, since I didn't want either of them myself. It was my transsexual complex—I was envious that I couldn't have what I wanted, what they could have with each other.

"That's why I'm convinced that Proust himself was the same way—an inverted transsexual. Because he had this pathological interest in lesbian relationships, and this pining for what he couldn't have. But he had to find a substitute, since he couldn't realize his true nature with women—

not with straight women and not with lesbians. So to compensate, he became 'gay.'

"He didn't really understand his orientation, of course. Other gay artists, when they describe young men, you can tell how much it moves them, but that doesn't happen with Proust. I'm one hundred percent convinced that he was not a normal gay man who was satisfied with his situation. He wanted something else, either consciously or subconsciously, but since that wasn't possible he found a sexual variation he could live with."

Because we often hung out together until late in the evening, Ksyusha and I frequently shared a bed at her apartment, or at mine, or at the dacha. These were narrow beds, and they forced us into an unavoidably intimate proximity. We'd cuddle gently; sometimes I got hard. An unspoken suggestion always lay between us.

One evening at her place she showed me all her old photographs, which she stored in envelopes of varied shapes and sizes. She recounted stories relating to each—her first female lover, a woman with pursed lips and a simpering sensuality; the slender, straggly man she almost married; Natasha, with whom she spent five years; Ksyusha herself, a gawky teenager with a marvelously malleable face.

As we lay in bed together that night, we talked about sex. She wondered why many gay men would not want to experience both active and passive positions; as for herself, she was curious to try using a dildo, but she didn't know where she could buy one in Moscow. I promised to bring her one from America, then mumbled the tentative proposition stumbling about in my mind.

"I, uh, I have this feeling that, uh…this desire to kiss you."

If the suggestion surprised her, she did not show it. "Now?"

"Yes."

She leaned toward me and, ever so slightly, parted her pale, plump lips. I brushed my own against them, and our tongues lingered for a taste of awkward sweetness. I did not probe deeper, not did Ksyusha; after some moments, she drew back and whispered good night. I felt relieved. Though I was then, and at other times, almost beside myself with feeling, we both seemed unwilling to breach the barrier that our respective sexual identities had imposed between us.

One spring evening, as we gathered around the dining room table at the dacha, Sveta suggested we play "Truth"—a game in which whoever refused to answer a personal question lost. We had just watched a movie on television about a woman, her husband, and her lover during the Russian Revolution, and "Truth" had figured explosively in the climax; one of the men admitted that he was a speculator, and the other denounced him to the authorities.

Our version was a lot tamer and got off to a slow start. At first, we all just stared at each other. Finally, Sveta turned to me. "How often do you wash your feet?" This question embarrassed me, since I had already gained a reputation as the slovenly American. There was no bath at the dacha, I replied, so I did not wash my feet there; although at my apartment in Moscow I did so once or twice a day.

"That wasn't very interesting," someone interjected. "Is that the best anyone can do?"

We sat and stared some more until I ventured a more challenging question. "Vitya, have you ever slept with a man?"

A small grin pierced his face. "No."

"But do you like kissing them?"

The grin cracked wider. "Yes. Because I like to kiss someone of whatever sex if I like the person. Still, with a man it is nice, but it is not a *sexual* feeling for me, the way it is with a woman."

The game continued. Guy, our British friend, asked Sveta about "the most golden" time of her life. "I like it when I am in love. I like that better than when someone is in love with me," she said. "Because then I think about what parts of myself I can use to catch them...and I always think of something. They always fall in love with me when I sing." She warbled a lilting tune that she claimed to have employed in wooing Lena, who fluttered her hands and coyly insisted she could not play the game.

"When people pressure me to tell the truth, I am physiologically incapable of it," Lena declared.

Sveta hooted. "Listen to that, I've given all these years of my life to this woman and now I learn she's psychologically incapable of telling the truth!"

"No, not psychologically," corrected Lena. "Physiologically, and only if someone tries to force me. But you all know me, if you ask me a question you can judge for yourself if it's the truth or not."

I noticed Vitya looking at me and prepared myself. "David...any erotic moments in your relationship with Ksyusha?"

I took a breath and glanced at her; her face was blank, immobile. "Well, yes, there's something there." I paused. "It's been fifteen years since I had sexual feelings for a woman, but there was one night at her house when we kissed. So, yes, those feelings are there, definitely."

Ksyusha looked at me. "I felt that...from your side."

Hot confusion gripped me. "And from yours?"

"No, I don't have those kinds of feelings for you." Her voice was flat and dry, like the whistle of a distant train. "If I had them, we would already have slept together. But it is enough for me, what we have. I don't want that with you."

My body stiffened. What she said hurt, and I was startled and annoyed at how much it hurt. The game dragged on, but I brooded over Ksyusha's remarks for the rest of the evening and into the next morning.

It was Sunday, a time for working the land. Ksyusha vigorously shoveled manure onto a patch of dirt, churning it to spread the nutrients evenly. Vitya was constructing a little greenhouse for growing tomatoes; he grunted and hauled heavy logs into place. Lena knelt down to clear a space for planting carrots and beets, her plump figure settling onto the ground like an upside-down light bulb. With her strong hands she raked the soil, tugging out suspicious growths and tossing them into the pail by her side.

As I watched them at their labors, a sullen mood gathered in my chest like a lump of cold, hard clay. I left the dacha late in the afternoon and returned to the apartment I shared with Kevin. There I found, to my irritation, a crowd: two American lesbians, three gays from Rostov-on-Don in southern Russia, other friends of Kevin's who I didn't want to see. I moped about, grumbled, barked at someone or other, complained about the dirty dishes scattered everywhere.

Then Ksyusha phoned. She, too, had returned to the city, she was with her friend Volodya, could they come over? I could tell from her voice that she had been drinking. "Ksyusha, there's already a batch of people staying here. There's only the floor left to sleep on."

"David, wait for us, we'll think of something. We'll be right over!"

She hung up. Oh, fuck! I wanted time to myself; I'd had it with these crazy Russians. Why couldn't they just let me be?

My bad humor was all about Ksyusha, of course, and her flip dismissal of what I'd admitted the night before. But when she and Volodya arrived, I ranted and raved about everything else—the throng at my apartment, the mess in the kitchen, my thwarted desire to be alone. My obvious distress triggered Ksyusha into action.

"David, David," she murmured, "I will stand in front of your door all night if I have to—all night, all night, do you hear?—and no one, *no one*, will disturb you because I am here. Don't worry, *Ksyusha* is here...."

This outpouring of tipsy maternal tenderness, so misguided yet thoroughly sincere, doused my anger in its wake. I laughed in spite of myself.

Kevin and his latest boyfriend emerged naked from his bedroom. Ksyusha, devoted guardian of my solitude, promptly invited them into my room to join us for a drink. The radio sputtered a mournful tune and she and I started to dance in slow, rhythmic waves. She pressed her body against mine and ran her hand under my shirt, up my spine; then she leaned her head back and offered up a drunken smile. "I hope you weren't upset yesterday when I said I wasn't attracted to you. I was too shy and embarrassed to confess it in front of everybody."

Relief spilled over me in a heavy sigh. I wrapped my arm around her. I was in love. "I didn't think it was true," I said bravely.

She laughed—that guttural drawl of hers that always prickled my skin. The music soared, and we danced some more in the swirling haze of soft light and smoke.

Kevin scrutinized us from his nude perch on the couch. "Hey, Dave, have you two gotten this over with and slept with each other yet?"

"We were just sort of discussing that topic," I said sheepishly.

"They really want each other," Kevin remarked, to no one in particular.

"That's right!" Ksyusha agreed, with the giddy clarity of the besotted.

But we didn't make love, that night or any other. I'm gay, I told myself. I have sex with men. The whole situation unnerved me—I wondered if my hypothalamus had grown or something. I entertained the fleeting thought that I should marry Ksyusha and bring her back to the United States, but I let that idea fade; she belonged here, not there. Only in Moscow, in Russia, could her essence survive.

Ksyusha had her own idea for why we never slept together. "When we met, we met in a gay context, at the conference," she once said. "And that meant for me that we wouldn't sleep together, that our friendship came first. Maybe if we met somewhere else, at an ecology conference or something, it would have developed on another path."

Ksyusha's offhand remark reminded me of the vast gulf between us. She was a dyke at the gay conference, but could be someone else elsewhere; my gay identity was with me always, at ecology conferences and on the subway, too, or while flossing my teeth. I admired and envied her ability to flow this way or that, to respond to the situation and, on occasion, shed her dykeness and try on another guise. And I was exhilarated to feel something that I had long ago dismissed—to discover that my sexuality was more nuanced and complex than I had assumed.

Still, I was afraid to smash the spell of our unconsummated passion. And ultimately, my attraction to men remained stronger, and more familiar—

as comfortable as a well-worn T-shirt. Thought I felt so much for her, I enjoyed the consistency of the gay identity I had forged out of the chaos of my childhood, its clarity and continuity. I had little desire to complicate my life, to relive the sexual struggle of my past.

Maybe that was an excuse; but it was the choice I made. Yet I realized that others might have made a different choice. I realized, too, what I should have always known: that sexuality is far more subtle than the rigid categories, the concrete bunkers, that we create to describe it; that there is no right or wrong way to be gay or lesbian or anything else; and that I had been arrogant, or stupid, to ever think that there might be.

Those insights might sound obvious and trite, and I had heard others express them before. But I had never really understood, or agreed—until I met Ksyusha and the dacha crowd.

For with no gay community to turn to, they created their own rules. The dacha was a self-contained world, a sexual greenhouse, where exotic variations flowered and thrived; my friends relied on the internal promptings and rhythms of their bodies and hearts, not on an ideology imposed from outside. They made it all up as they lived their lives.

That was a skill I had forgotten, or never had in the first place. I learned it at the dacha.

About The Authors

Dorothy Allison is the author of *Bastard Out of Carolina*, a National Book Award Finalist; *Two or Three Things I Know For Sure; Trash*, winner of two Lambda Literary awards; *The Women Who Hate Me;* and *Skin: Talking About Sex, Class, and Literature*, winner of the Lambda Literary Award. She lives in Northern California with her partner Alix and son Wolf.

Laura Antoniou is the editor of many anthologies, including *Leatherwomen I* and *II, Looking for Mr. Preston, By Her Subdued, No Greater Tribute, Some Women,* and the forthcoming *Tales of the Marketplace* and *Leatherwomen III*. Under the name Sara Adamson she is the author of *The Catalyst* and *The Marketplace Trilogy (The Marketplace, The Slave,* and *The Trainer)*. Under the name Christopher Morgan, she wrote the gay male erotic novel *Musclebound* and the collection of erotic gay male stories, *Steam Gauge and Other Tales,* and edited the anthology *Sportsmen* and, for its brief existence, the gay male porn magazine, *The Badboy Magazine*. Several of her books have been translated into German, Japanese and Korean. She lives in New York City.

Pat Califia is a troublemaker, and for many years has been defying boundaries with regard to stereotypes of gender and erotic writings. She is the author of *Sex Changes: The Politics of Transgenderism* and *Public Sex: The Culture of Radical Sex* (both from Cleis Press). For many years, she wrote a sex advice column for gay men that ran in *The Advocate, Advocate Classifieds,* and other periodicals. She is the editor of *Doing it for Daddy, The Lesbian S/M Safety Manual, Coming to Power,* and *The Second Coming,* and the author of *Macho Sluts, Melting Point, Doc and Fluff, Sapphistry, The Advocate Adviser, The Sexpert,* and other books. She lives in San Francisco.

Greta Christina is managing editor of the online sex magazine *Fishnet* (www.blowfish.com/fishnet). She is also film critic for the *Spectator* and book critic for San Francisco *Frontiers*. Her work has appeared in *Penthouse, Ms.,* and *On Our Backs,* as well as the anthologies *The Erotic Impulse* and *Bisexual Politics: Theories, Queries and Visions.* She enjoys books, films, food, weird music, weird sex, reference materials, and writing about herself in the third person.

Michael Thomas Ford is the author of more than twenty books, including *The Voices of AIDS, Alec Baldwin Doesn't Love Me and Other Trials of My Queer Life, OutSpoken,* and *The World Out There: Becoming Part of the Lesbian and Gay Community.* He is editor of *Best Gay Erotica 1996, Once Upon a Time: Erotic Fairy Tales for Women,* and *Happily Ever After: Erotic Fairy Tales for Men,* among others, and his own fiction and essays have appeared in numerous collections.

Jill Nagle is editor of *Whores and Other Feminists* (Routledge). She lives in San Francisco. Engaged in an ongoing series of experiments with gender, sex, theory, and social justice, her work has also been published in *Closer to Home: Bisexuality and Feminism* (under the pseudonym Vashti Zabatinsky), *Bisexual Politics: Theories, Queries and Visions,* and *First Person Sexual.*

Katherine Raymond was born on April 21, 1974, the scion of a long line of lesbians and Assyrian Orthodox priests (not together). She currently resides in Brooklyn, New York, where she designs and programs Web pages, and is an astrologer, editor, and cultural critic. Her fiendish plan for world domination is outlined in detail at http://apokrypha.com.

D. Travers Scott is the author of *Execution, Texas: 1987* (St. Martin's) and the editor of *Strategic Sex* (Cleis Press). His writing and performance work have appeared in *Harper's, Best Gay Erotica 1996* and *1997, Best American Gay Fiction 1997, Switch Hitters, Southern Comfort, Drummer, Steam,* and *Reclaiming the Heartland,* among other periodicals and anthologies.

David Tuller is a journalist who works for the *San Francisco Chronicle.* "Adventures of a Dacha Sex Spy" is adapted from his book *Cracks in the Iron Closet* (Faber & Faber hardcover/University of Chicago Press paperback).

Marco Vassi was a literary avatar of the sexual revolution. He was deeply attuned to the politics of sex and sexual orientation, as well as the intersections of sex and spirituality. In his writing, as in his life (until his AIDS diagnosis), he explored fearlessly, bringing back dispatches from sexual frontiers most people never visited. Less well-known in the queer community than he deserves to be, Vassi died in the mid-1980s. His large body of work includes the books *The Erotic Comedies, The Stoned Apocalypse, The Saline Solution, Slave Lover, A Driving Passion, The Devil's Sperm Is Cold,* and *Contours of Darkness,* among many others.

John Weir is author of the novel *The Irreversible Decline of Edie Socket,* which won a Lambda Literary Award. He lives in New York and has written for *Outweek, Details,* and *The Advocate,* among many other periodicals.

Riki Anne Wilchins is a lesbian or bisexual, transsexual or transgender, man or woman living in Greenwich Village or New York City and is the author of *Read My Lips! Sexual Subversion and the End of Gender* (Firebrand). Her hobbies include the Transexual Menace, the Lesbian Avengers, and attacking false binaries or any other political system which oppresses her or just really pisses her off. She is a founding member of the Transexual Menace and current Executive Director of GenderPAC.

ABOUT THE EDITORS

Carol Queen is the author of *The Leatherdaddy and the Femme* (Cleis Press, forthcoming 1998), *Real Live Nude Girl: Chronicles of Sex-Positive Culture* (Cleis Press) and *Exhibitionism for the Shy* (Down There Press). A second novel, a collection of short stories, and more sex education material are in the works. Her erotic stories have appeared in *Best Gay Erotica 1996, Best American Erotica 1993* and *1994, Doing It For Daddy, Looking for Mr. Preston, Herotica 2, 3,* and *4, Virgin Territory, Leatherwomen, Noirotica, Coming Up: The World's Best Erotic Writing,* and *Once Upon a Time: Erotic Fairy Tales for Women.* Her essays about sex and culture have appeared in *The Erotic Impulse, Madonnarama, Women of The Light, Dagger, Bi Any Other Name, The Second Coming,* and *Bisexual Politics: Theories, Queries and Visions.* She has contributed to such 'zines and journals as *Taste of Latex, Frighten the Horses, Libido, Slippery When Wet, Black Sheets, The Realist, P-Form, The Advocate, Girljock, The Insurgent Sociologist,* and *The San Francisco Bay Guardian,* and a monthly column in the Bay Area sex newspaper *Spectator.* She lives in San Francisco, is a worker/owner at Good Vibrations, and is pursuing a doctorate in sexology.

Lawrence Schimel is the author of *The Drag Queen of Elfland* (The Ultra Violet Library) and editor of more than twenty anthologies, including *Switch Hitters: Lesbians Write Gay Male Erotica and Gay Men Write Lesbian Erotica* (with Carol Queen; Cleis Press); *Food For Life and Other Dish* (Cleis Press); *Two Hearts Desire: Gay Couples on Their Love* (with Michael Lassell, St. Martin's Press); *The Mammoth Book of Gay Erotica* (Caroll & Graf); and the forthcoming *Kosher Meat* (Cleis Press), among others. His short fiction, essays, and poetry have appeared in over one hundred anthologies, including *Best Gay Erotica 1997, The Random House Book of Science Fiction Stories, Ritual Sex, Weird Tales From Shakespeare,* and *The Random House Treasury of Light Verse,* among others, as well as in numerous periodicals, ranging from *Drummer* to *Cricket.* He lives in Manhattan, where he writes and edits full time.

Also by Carol Queen & Lawrence Schimel

Switch Hitters

Lesbians Write Gay Male Erotica and Gay Men Write Lesbian Erotica

Can hot gay porn flow from the pens of lesbian writers? Can gay men write convincingly of lesbian sex? Switch Hitters twists our gender expectations in these provocative sex stories by gold star authors from across the Kinsey spectrum: Pat Califia, Matthew Rettenmund, Carol Queen, Kevin Killian, Blake C. Aarens, Thomas Roche, Jenne Blade, William J. Mann, Robin Sweeney, Marco Vassi, Cecilia Tan, Larry Townsend, Wickie Stamps, Simon Sheppard, Laura Antoniou, Lawrence Schimel, Lucy Taylor, D. Travers Scott.

"This is the stuff of genderfuck and solidarity, curiosity and cultural appropriation, and it makes a peculiar kind of sense that queer boys and girls would be trying on each other's sexual realities for size."

— Carol Queen and Lawrence Schimel, from the Introduction

Praise for Switch Hitters

"...one of the most conceptually interesting collections—sexual or otherwise." —*HX Magazine*

"...a great collection of gay and lesbian erotica: the men and women of Switch Hitters prove they can write — and write well — of each others' sexual realities." — *Paramour*

"Carol Queen and Lawrence Schimel take genderfuck to a new level..." — Loraine Hutchins, *Lambda Book Report*

"...tour de force book of erotic tales." — *Bay Windows*

Erotica/Gay & Lesbian Studies/Gender Studies
194 pages
ISBN: 1-57344-021-3
$12.95

Call to order:
Cleis Press 1-800-780-2279

Real Live Nude Girl
Chronicles of Sex-Positive Culture
by Carol Queen

I bought my first brassiere in thirteen years. I grew my hair; I wore
skirts; I put on lipstick. The white lace that I'd squirreled away for my
lover's delectation I began to wear in public. I mixed it with leather. My
lovers began to get nervous. I hoped to become so outré that no one
would notice, or care, what I did.

In the peep show I was privileged to see secret visions of sexual desire
and fantasy played out over and over again; I knew I had a front-row seat
at one usually-hidden aspect of sexual culture. Besides, the peep show is a
microcosm of eroticism, desire, persona, the theatrical ritual of fantasy, and
the very same sexual schizophrenia that creates the climate for peep shows
in the first place. The peeps are a rich stew, and I want to stir it in public.

"It's apparent to anyone who reads Carol Queen's work that she com-
bines a powerful intellectual persona and an astonishing sexual persona
in everything she writes." — *Spectator*

"The thinking person's sex queen, Carol Queen is a real live *brilliant*
girl. For people who can't imagine what all the fuss is about sex, this is
the book to read." — Annie Sprinkle, Pleasure Activist/Artist

Carol Queen is "…heiress apparent to the mantle currently worn by
the indispensable Susie Bright: all-American, bisexual pleasure polemi-
cist, and erotic essayist. " — *Amazon.com*

Gay & Lesbian Studies/Bisexuality
200 pages
ISBN: 1-57344-073-6
$14.95

Call to order:
Cleis Press 1-800-780-2279

BOOKS FROM CLEIS PRESS

Gender Transgression

Body Alchemy: Transsexual Portraits
by Loren Cameron.
Lambda Literary Award Winner.
ISBN: 1-57344-062-0 24.95 paper.

Dagger: On Butch Women,
edited by Roxxie, Lily Burana,
Linnea Due.
ISBN: 0-939416-82-4 14.95 paper.

*I Am My Own Woman: The
Outlaw Life
of Charlotte von Mahlsdorf,*
translated by Jean Hollander.
ISBN: 1-57344-010-8 12.95 paper.

*PoMoSexuals: Challenging
Assumptions about Gender
and Sexuality*
edited by Carol Queen
and Lawrence Schimel.
Preface by Kate Bornstein.
ISBN: 1-57344-074-4 14.95 paper.

*Sex Changes: The Politics of
Transgenderism*
by Pat Califia
ISBN: 1-57344-072-8 16.95 paper.

*Switch Hitters: Lesbians Write Gay
Male Erotica and Gay Men Write
Lesbian Erotica,*
edited by Carol Queen
and Lawrence Schimel.
ISBN: 1-57344-021-3 12.95 paper.

Sexual Politics

*Forbidden Passages:
Writings Banned in Canada,*
introductions by Pat Califia
and Janine Fuller.
Lambda Literary Award Winner.
ISBN: 1-57344-019-1 14.95 paper.

*Public Sex:
The Culture of Radical Sex*
by Pat Califia.
ISBN: 0-939416-89-1 12.95 paper.

*Real Live Nude Girl:
Chronicles of Sex-Positive Culture*
by Carol Queen.
ISBN: 1-57344-073-6. 14.95 paper.

*Sex Work: Writings by Women in
the Sex Industry,*
edited by Frédérique Delacoste
and Priscilla Alexander.
ISBN: 0-939416-11-5 16.95 paper.

*Susie Bright's Sexual Reality:
A Virtual Sex World Reader*
by Susie Bright.
ISBN: 0-939416-59-X 9.95 paper.

Susie Bright's Sexwise
by Susie Bright.
ISBN: 1-57344-002-7 10.95 paper.

Susie Sexpert's Lesbian Sex World
by Susie Bright.
ISBN: 0-939416-35-2 9.95 paper.

Erotic Literature

Best Gay Erotica 1998,
selected by Christopher Bram,
edited by Richard Labonté.
ISBN: 1-57344-031-0 14.95 paper.

Best Gay Erotica 1997,
selected by Douglas Sadownick,
edited by Richard Labonté.
ISBN: 1-57344-067-1 14.95 paper.

Best Gay Erotica 1996,
selected by Scott Heim,
edited by Michael Ford.
ISBN: 1-57344-052-3 12.95 paper.

Best Lesbian Erotica 1998,
selected by Jenifer Levin,
edited by Tristan Taormino.
ISBN: 1-57344-032-9 14.95 paper.

Best Lesbian Erotica 1997,
selected by Jewelle Gomez,
edited by Tristan Taormino.
ISBN: 1-57344-065-5 14.95 paper.

*Serious Pleasure: Lesbian Erotic
Stories and Poetry,*
edited by the Sheba Collective.
ISBN: 0-939416-45-X 9.95 paper.

Lesbian and Gay Studies

*The Case of the Good-For-Nothing
Girlfriend*
by Mabel Maney.
Lambda Literary Award
Nominee.
ISBN: 0-939416-91-3 10.95 paper.

The Case of the Not-So-Nice Nurse
by Mabel Maney.
Lambda Literary Award Nominee.
ISBN: 0-939416-76-X 9.95 paper.

*Nancy Clue and the Hardly Boys in
A Ghost in the Closet*
by Mabel Maney.
Lambda Literary Award Nominee.
ISBN: 1-57344-012-4 10.95 paper.

*Different Daughters:
A Book by Mothers of Lesbians,*
second edition,
edited by Louise Rafkin.
ISBN: 1-57344-050-7 12.95 paper.

*Different Mothers:
Sons & Daughters of Lesbians Talk
about Their Lives,*
edited by Louise Rafkin.
Lambda Literary Award Winner.
ISBN: 0-939416-41-7 9.95 paper.

A Lesbian Love Advisor
by Celeste West.
ISBN: 0-939416-26-3 9.95 paper.

On the Rails: A Memoir,
second edition,
by Linda Niemann.
Introduction by
Leslie Marmon Silko.
ISBN: 1-57344-064-7. 14.95 paper.

Queer Dog: Homo Pup Poetry,
edited by
Gerry Gomez Pearlberg.
ISBN: 1-57344-071-X. 12.95. paper.

Sex Guides

*Good Sex: Real Stories
from Real People,*
second edition,
by Julia Hutton.
ISBN: 1-57344-000-0 14.95 paper.

*The New Good Vibrations Guide to Sex:
Tips and techniques from America's
favorite sex-toy store,* second edition,
by Cathy Winks
and Anne Semans.
ISBN. 1-57344-069 8 21.95 paper

*The Ultimate Guide to Anal Sex
for Women*
by Tristan Taormino.
ISBN: 1-57344-028-0 14.95 paper.

Debut Fiction

Memory Mambo
by Achy Obejas.
Lambda Literary Award Winner.
ISBN: 1-57344-017-5 12.95 paper.

*We Came All The Way from Cuba
So You Could Dress Like This?:*
Stories by Achy Obejas.
Lambda Literary Award Nominee.
ISBN: 0-939416-93-X 10.95 paper.

Seeing Dell
by Carol Guess
ISBN: 1-57344-023-X 12.95 paper.

World Literature

A Forbidden Passion
by Cristina Peri Rossi.
ISBN: 0 939416-68-9 9 95 paper.

*Half a Revolution: Contemporary
Fiction by Russian Women,*
edited by Masha Gessen.
ISBN 1-57344-006-X $12.95 paper.

*The Little School: Tales of
Disappearance and Survival
in Argentina*
by Alicia Partnoy.
ISBN: 0-939416-07-7 9.95 paper.

Peggy Deery: An Irish Family at War
by Nell McCafferty.
ISBN: 0-939416-39-5 9.95 paper.

Thrillers & Dystopias

Another Love
by Erzsébet Galgóczi.
ISBN: 0-939416-51-4 8.95 paper.

Dirty Weekend: A Novel of Revenge
by Helen Zahavi.
ISBN: 0-939416-85-9 10.95 paper.

Only Lawyers Dancing
by Jan McKemmish.
ISBN: 0-939416-69-7 9.95 paper.

The Wall
by Marlen Haushofer.
ISBN: 0-939416-54-9 9.95 paper.

Vampires & Horror

*Brothers of the Night:
Gay Vampire Stories*
edited by Michael Rowe
and Thomas S. Roche.
ISBN: 1-57344-025-6 14.95 paper.

Dark Angels:
Lesbian Vampire Stories,
edited by Pam Keesey.
Lambda Literary Award Nominee.
ISBN 1-7344-014-0 10.95 paper.

Daughters of Darkness:
Lesbian Vampire Stories,
edited by Pam Keesey.
ISBN: 0-939416-78-6 9.95 paper.

Vamps: An Illustrtated History
of the Femme Fatale
by Pam Keesey.
ISBN: 1-57344-026-4 21.95.

Sons of Darkness: Tales of Men,
Blood and Immortality,
edited by Michael Rowe
and Thomas S. Roche.
Lambda Literary Award Nominee.
ISBN: 1-57344-059-0 12.95 paper.

Women Who Run with the
Werewolves: Tales of Blood, Lust
and Metamorphosis,
edited by Pam Keesey.
Lambda Literary Award Nominee.
ISBN: 1-57344-057-4 12.95 paper.

Politics of Health
The Absence of the Dead Is Their
Way of Appearing
by Mary Winfrey Trautmann.
ISBN: 0-939416-04-2 8.95 paper.

Don't: A Woman's Word
by Elly Danica.
ISBN: 0-939416-22-0 8.95 paper

Voices in the Night: Women
Speaking About Incest,
edited by Toni A.H. McNaron and
Yarrow Morgan.
ISBN: 0-939416-02-6 9.95 paper.

With the Power of Each Breath:
A Disabled Women's Anthology,
edited by Susan Browne,
Debra Connors and Nanci Stern.
ISBN: 0-939416-06-9 10.95 paper.

Comix
Dyke Strippers:
Lesbian Cartoonists A to Z,
edited by Roz Warren.
ISBN: 1-57344-008-6 16.95 paper.

The Night Audrey's Vibrator Spoke:
A Stonewall Riots Collection
by Andrea Natalie.
Lambda Literary Award Nominee.
ISBN: 0-939416-64-6 8.95 paper.

Revenge of Hothead Paisan:
Homicidal Lesbian Terrorist
by Diane DiMassa.
Lambda Literary Award Nominee.
ISBN: 1-57344-016-7 16.95 paper.

Travel & Cooking
Betty and Pansy's Severe Queer
Review of New York
by Betty Pearl and Pansy.
ISBN: 1-57344-070-1 10.95 paper.

Betty and Pansy's Severe Queer Review
of San Francisco
by Betty Pearl and Pansy.
ISBN: 1-57344-056-6 10.95 paper.

Food for Life & Other Dish,
edited by Lawrence Schimel.
ISBN: 1-57344-061-2 14.95 paper.

Writer's Reference
Putting Out: The Essential
Publishing Resource Guide For
Gay and Lesbian Writers,
fourth edition,
by Edisol W. Dotson.
ISBN: 1-57344-033-7 14.95 paper.

Since 1980, Cleis Press has published provocative, smart books —
for girlfriends of all genders. Cleis Press books are easy to find at your
favorite bookstore — or direct from us! We welcome your order and
will ship your books as quickly as possible. Individual orders must be
prepaid (U.S. dollars only). Please add 15% shipping. CA residents add
8.5% sales tax. MasterCard and Visa orders: include account number,
exp. date, and signature.

How to Order
- **Phone:** 1-800-780-2279 or (415) 575-4700
  Monday - Friday, 9 am - 5 pm Pacific Standard Time
- **Fax:** (415) 575-4705
- **Mail:** Cleis Press P.O. Box 14684, San Francisco, California 94114
- **E-mail:** Cleis@aol.com